THEY HAD TO GO OUT...

TRUE STORIES OF AMERICA'S COASTAL LIFE-SAVERS FROM THE PAGES OF "WRECK & RESCUE JOURNAL"

FOREWORD BY FREDERICK STONEHOUSE

Avery Color Studios, Inc.
Gwinn, Michigan

United States Life-Saving Service Heritage Association
Hull, Massachusetts

ISBN-13: 978-1-892384-39-3
ISBN-10: 1-892384-39-6

Library of Congress Control Number: 2006931408

First Edition–2007
10 9 8 7 6 5 4 3 2 1

Published by Avery Color Studios, Inc.
Gwinn, Michigan 49841

Cover photos: top photo courtesy of the U.S. Coast Guard,
bottom photo courtesy of the Richard Small Collection
Back cover photo: courtesy of the Hull Historical Society

T 64124

Association Information:

**The United States Life-Saving Service
Heritage Association**
P.O. Box 213
Hull, Massachusetts 02045
www.us-lifesavingservice.org

TABLE OF CONTENTS

•• •• --- ••   •• •• --- ••   •• •• --- ••   •• •• --- ••   •• •• --- ••

•• •• --- •• ••

• • • – – • • •

FOREWORD

••• --- •••   ••• --- •••   ••• --- •••

by Frederick Stonehouse

THEY were unique in American history. Nothing like them ever existed before or since. In more than 30 years of maritime historical research no organization has impressed me more than the old U.S. Life-Saving Service. I kind of backed into the USLSS. I always knew about Coast Guard rescue work. Growing up on the New Jersey shore in the 1950s I often saw the local crew drive their "DUKW" into the surf.[1] When I began to research shipwrecks I frequently ran across stories of USLSS involvement, leading me to follow-up on their overall role in the maritime world. The more I discovered, the more I wanted to know and it wasn't long before I was hooked on this remarkable organization.

The men of the old U.S. Life-Saving Service defined courage. They bled valor. Their unofficial motto: "Regulations say we have to go out, they say nothing about coming back," wasn't an organizational "mission statement" as used today. It was simply the way they lived and died! If ever the old phrase, "wooden ships and iron men" applied, it was to the men of the USLSS.

Time and again, these "storm warriors" and "heroes of the surf" launched their small boats into crashing wave and screaming wind, not for personal gain or glory but for the satisfaction of saving lives of shipwrecked mariners and passengers.

At one point in their illustrious career surfmen were paid a lousy 93 cents a day and from it they had to cover the cost of uniforms and rations. And it was seasonal employment without the guarantee of work the following year. There was no retirement, disability pay or death gratuity "from a grateful nation."

••• --- •••

1

If the pay was so bad, why did the men join? What prompted them to become part of such a benefits poor organization?

I submit it was the chance to be part of something special; an organization that set the performance bar high and demanded the men reach it. When Vince Lombardi said, "winning isn't everything. It is the only thing" it was a sports directed statement. For the men of the USLSS, "winning" meant saving lives, not just scoring touchdowns.

Failure wasn't tolerated. For example, when the wreck was "going to pieces on the bar" and a storm raged full and hard, regulations demanded the keeper launch the boats. A simple look at surf conditions and a hasty determination it was "too rough" wasn't acceptable. He had to try! If the waves beat him back he tried again. If plainly the boat wasn't the answer he had to try something else. Quitting wasn't an answer. Failure to make every effort to make a rescue meant dismissal for keeper and crew. Danger wasn't an excuse for not trying. Unlike today the rottenness of political correctness had no place. You didn't get special preference for being a minority, physically handicapped or female. "Points" for trying didn't count. It was results that mattered. Lives were at stake.

No Life-Saving crew ever did a "risk analysis" before going to a rescue. No life-saving crew ever "dead-lined" a boat because the crew wasn't "qualified" to launch. It was the job of the keeper to train his men and since he was the coxswain too, his life was also on the line. Regulations held the keeper personally responsible for the efficiency of his men.

There weren't any fancy equipment or inches thick "qualification" standards and manuals. Instead they had old-fashioned training, experience, dedication and local knowledge. The USLSS crews were also intensely local. A man could spend his entire career at the same station or perhaps transfer to one a dozen miles distant. The benefit was a vast knowledge of local conditions, vital to make rescues under near impossible situations. They knew the reefs, shoals, sandbars and currents. It also meant the crews were very interdependent, within the crew and with the crews up and down the coast. They were part of a strong team, at the station and district level. A major criticism of today's Coast Guard is the rapid turnover and transfer of crewmen at the boat stations creating a constant aura of confusion and a lack of cohesion.

Times do change however and the U.S. Life-Saving Service and Revenue Marine merged in 1915 to form today's Coast Guard. 1915 marks the true start of the Coast Guard combining the deep-sea cruising traditions of Revenue Marine and USLSS inshore rescue. Its' a winning combination for America.

For a time the rich traditions of the USLSS continued in the new Coast Guard but over time the old standards and ethics faded away. No longer did iron men take wood boats into the surf regardless of the odds. An era passed. A new one began.

The two photos from the front cover speak volumes of the steadfastness of the old lifesavers. The bearded man with all the medals is Joshua James, probably the most celebrated lifesaver in the world credited with saving hundreds of lives from the age of 15 when he first joined the Massachusetts Humane Society until his death in 1902. He was honored with the highest medals for valor of the Humane Society, the United States, and many other organizations. Originally with the Massachusetts Humane Society station at Hull, at age 62 he was appointed to the USLSS. He died on March 1902 after putting his crew through several hours of surfboat drill during a howling northeast gale. James fully knew the value of great training under realistic and demanding conditions. Upon grounding the boat on the beach he nimbly jumped onto the wet sand, glanced at the sea and stated, "The tide is ebbing," and promptly dropped dead on the beach! He was 75 years old and a lifesaver to the very last!

The man handling the sweep oar on the surfboat is George W. Plough, one of the legendary keepers of the Great Lakes. Richard M. Small, later a storied keeper in his own right, is one of the crewmen. Keepers usually came up through the ranks, serving time as a surfman before taking the awesome responsibility of keeper. USLSS leaders came from the bottom up, earning their way to the sweep oar.

In the technically sophisticated age we live in today, filled with electronic wizardry of all kinds, it is important we remember the men of the old Life-Saving Service. Their steadfast courage, devotion to duty and refusal to quit trying can be an inspiration to us all.

¹The DUKW (DUCK) is a six-wheel-drive amphibious truck developed by the United States during World War II for hauling material and troops over land and water and for approaching and crossing beaches in amphibious attacks.

DUKWs were used in landings in the Pacific, in North Africa, and on the D-Day beaches of Normandy. D indicates a vehicle designed in 1942, the U means "utility (amphibious)", the K indicates all-wheel drive and the W two powered rear axles. The hybrid was crafted around a conventional six-wheel-drive military truck called the CCKW, with the addition of a watertight hull and a propeller.

Following the war the many DUKWs found their way into Coast Guard beach stations where they proved useful navigating the dunes and making short run rescues in fairly calm conditions.

INTRODUCTION

JUST a little more than a decade ago, the country's leading Coast Guard historians – specifically those men and women interested in the story of the United States Life-Saving Service – gathered on the Cape Cod National Seashore to discuss the current status and future of the vanishing architecture, artifacts and, most importantly, history of the early Coast Guard. The task seemed overwhelming: could they save a significant cultural resource on a national scale before it was lost forever? They decided that even if they couldn't do that, as, for instance, more than half of the lifesaving stations built in the Life-Saving Service years (1848, 1871 or 1878-1915, based on different theories) had already disappeared, they would at least go down trying, and doing so together.

From that small grouping of historians, writers, National Park Service interpreters and museum professionals came two fertile ideas. First, they would form a national nonprofit organization, based in Massachusetts, the United States Life-Saving Service Heritage Association, to "preserve the stations, history, boats and equipment of the U.S. Life-Saving Service and U.S. Coast Guard." Second, they voted to create a quarterly publication, *Wreck & Rescue Journal*, to keep alive the stories of the surfmen and keepers that manned lifeboats, rigged breeches buoys, and otherwise did whatever they could to save mariners in distress at sea.

But that was in 1995. So what happened?

Today, the United States Life-Saving Service Heritage Association is stronger than ever, receiving Congressional recognition at its tenth annual meeting, held at the Sleeping Bear Dunes National Lakeshore in Leelanau

County, Michigan, for ten years of work in historic preservation. *Wreck & Rescue* is read in Coast Guard stations all over America and is sent across our northern border to Canada, overseas to readers in England, and has even been carried by U.S. Coast Guard representatives to their equivalents in China. In ten years, the *Journal* has doubled in size from 16 to 32 pages, allowing for more, longer scholarly articles about the history of search and rescue operations in the United States and around the world. The stories told in this book, the first ever compilation of the best writing from the *Journal*, represent only a small portion of the work of the most talented Coast Guard historians in the U.S. today

In these pages you will read work by Great Lakes authors like Frederick Stonehouse, author of numerous books on the maritime history of that region, including *Wreck Ashore: The United States Life-Saving Service on the Great Lakes*; tales of heroism and heartbreak by West Coast historians like Ralph Shanks, coauthor of *The United States Life-Saving Service: Heroes, Rescues and Architecture of the Early Coast Guard*, and Dennis Noble, author of, among others, *That Others Might Live: The United States Life-Saving Service, 1878-1914*, both of whom have made major national contributions to the history of search and rescue operations; first person accounts of life in the Coast Guard; specialized articles on the equipment used by the lifesavers; and much more. Geographically, these tales reach from northwest Washington to the choppy waters off downeast Maine to the treacherous Outer Banks of North Carolina. Chronologically, they stretch from the formation of the Humane Society of the Commonwealth of Massachusetts in 1786 to the late 1990s, from wooden pulling boats to modern 47-foot motor lifeboats.

Yet the story of the success of the U.S. Life-Saving Service Heritage Association does not end with the quarterly publication of *Wreck & Rescue Journal*. The true strength of the organization rests with its membership, men and women from around the country dedicated to keeping this history alive. Some are descendants of surfmen, some own old stations, some grew up in Coast Guard towns, and still others are just drawn to the tales of bravery inherent in the Coast Guard story. Whatever the reasons, they share a common passion.

That passion is exercised – literally – each fall, when the members of the organization gather at a different historically-rich area of the country to continue the discussion started at the first annual meeting: what can we do to save the lifesavers' story? In ten years' time U.S.L.S.S.H.A. has met on the Cape Cod National Seashore, on the Outer Banks, and at Sleeping Bear

Dunes. They've spent an extended weekend on Nantucket, in and around Bath and Portland, Maine, on Wisconsin's Door Peninsula, in southern New Jersey, at Marquette on Michigan's Upper Peninsula, and at the mouth of the Columbia River at Astoria, Oregon.

During the 2001 meeting in Scituate, Massachusetts, attendees rode Coast Guard boats from Station Point Allerton to America's oldest light station, Boston Light. They've climbed the South Manitou Lighthouse in Lake Michigan and sailed West Grand Traverse Bay on the schooner *Madeline*. In New Jersey their heads spun as they reached the dizzying heights of Cape May Lighthouse and Atlantic City's Absecon Lighthouses. In the Pacific Northwest they've joined the Coast Guard on 47-foot motor lifeboats on the Columbia River Bar, the most dangerous stretch of water in the world. They've met with active Coast Guardsmen and women at small boat stations on canals, lakeshores and seashores; witnessed rescue demonstrations by HH-65 Dolphin helicopters training with small boat crews; and marched in the footsteps of the surfmen that once walked America's shoreline, lanterns in hand, vigilantly searching the horizon for lives to save.

And the story will continue, as the surface has barely been scratched. There have been preservation successes and failure, but all along the way there has been a constant push to educate the public as to the amazing stories of the Coast Guard's past. And, the fact is, the history of the surfmen and keepers of old is rewritten on a daily basis, as today's Coast Guardsmen and women embody the spirit, ethic and courage that drove the lifesavers of yore to do the incredible work they did.

You will read a sentence in this book that is credited with being the traditional motto of search and rescue professionals of the past, "They had to go out, they did not have to come back." Today's lifesavers use Semper Paratus, or "Always Prepared" as their creed, but the effect is nearly the same. While they do the work they do, the members of the U.S. Life-Saving Service Heritage Association have also pledged to be prepared to react at a moments notice to do whatever is necessary to carry the Coast Guard story forward into the future. Perhaps after reading this book, you'll be ready to join them.

John Galluzzo,
Editor, *Wreck & Rescue Journal*

THE LIFESAVERS

Joshua James and the Portland Gale of November 1898

by John J. Galluzzo (Volume 3, Number 1)

IF Joshua James took time to reminisce when he arose the morning of Saturday, November 26, 1898, he would have realized that that day marked the tenth anniversary of his finest moment, the Great Storm of 1888, in which he and the volunteer Massachusetts Humane Society lifesavers of Hull, Massachusetts, rescued 29 men from six vessels within the span of about 36 hours. The crews that day committed the surfboat *Nantasket* to its first test, and she performed admirably enough to silence the experts who said she would never succeed as a lifesaving craft. The dramatic events of November 25-26, 1888, made Joshua James and the surfboat *Nantasket* the most famous lifesaving tandem in the world.

Now, ten years later, Joshua James, who had just turned 72 years old four days earlier on November 22, proudly wore the mantle of Keeper at the Point Allerton U.S. Life-Saving Service Station in Hull. The *Nantasket* rested quietly halfway down the beach in the Mass Humane Society station number 20. This station was the headquarters for Hull's volunteer crews, watched over by its Keeper, 33-year-old Osceola James, Joshua's only surviving son.

The year 1898 had been a busy one for Hull's lifesavers. January and February floods had wreaked havoc along the shores, stranding vessels and chasing townspeople to higher ground. During one rescue Keeper James attempted to walk across a frozen harbor to an ice-bound schooner, but plunged into the frigid waters after only a few steps. On January 31 the old-timers in town declared that day's storm to be the worst in living memory. To top it all off, the surfmen walking the short patrol to Pemberton Point claimed

When the Portland Gale ended, ships lay stewn across the northeast, some fully intact, others blown to pieces. Hull Historical Society

for two weeks straight that they were being visited by a ghost in the darkness beneath Battery Heights.

The outbreak of the Spanish-American War led to extra duty for the keeper and four of his surfmen as they received orders to remain on duty for the summer months and watch the horizon for enemy warships.

That summer the worst hailstorm in the town's history struck in mid-August, breaking three thousand panes of glass, and grounding a pleasure vessel on Toddy Rocks. On September 7, Joshua's beloved older sister Catherine Mathews, who had raised him after his mother died, passed away at 76 years old.

The first frost arrived in early November, but the month had otherwise been calm. The morning of the 26th seemed no different than the rest – seasonably chilly, breezy and cloudy. By late afternoon, though, the winds started to howl a bit stronger, and dark clouds began to gather overhead. By 7:00 p.m. snow began to fall, and by 11:30 the wind speed had reached 72 miles per hour. By midnight, the storm that would forever be known as the Portland Gale raged with all its fury.

Keeper Joshua James knew that a number of coal barges had dropped anchor in the harbor. At the first sign of trouble the tugboats pulling them left the barges with their crews on board to ride out the storms where they were, while the tugs headed for shelter. In November, just before the onset of winter, coal barges routinely followed the coast from Pennsylvania up into Boston Harbor to stock the city with the much-needed fuel. At midnight, approximately 15,000 tons of coal sat on vessels in the waters surrounding Hull. Within twelve hours it would all be on the sea floor.

At 3 a.m. patrolling surfman Fernando Bearse spotted a three-masted schooner a quarter of a mile out, directly in front of the station. As the surf was pounding so heavily and the wind was blowing so hard, the keeper decided against launching any boat just yet. About an hour later the vessel had been swept a third of a mile westward, now about 500 yards offshore. At daybreak, around 6:30, she, the *Henry R. Tilton*, had come within range of the station's Lyle gun. Volunteer lifesavers joined the crew on the way to the wreck, and the local Methodist pastor even came out to help, supplying coffee to the crew on the beach, one of whom was his son.

After two unsuccessful shots by Captain James, a third landed within reach of the sailors on board, who secured the whipline to the foremast twenty feet above the deck. After bringing the first man ashore, the Captain and his men realized that due to the fact that the vessel was still drifting shoreward, they would have to reset the lines, make them taut again. In order to keep the lines clear of debris, the men handling the lines had to stand dangerously close to the breaking waves, and from time to time the sea would engulf the surfmen and their equipment. It took over three hours, but the mixed crew of the government's hired men and the town's volunteers brought all seven mariners aboard to safety, resetting their lines between each rescue.

The Point Allerton life-saving crew's first test during the storm came with the stranding of the schooner Henry R. Tilton. *Hull Historical Society*

By the time Joshua and his "boys" had finished with their rescue efforts on the *Tilton*, word had already arrived that Consolidated Coal Company's Barge *#1* was dragging ashore on Toddy Rocks, three-quarters of a mile to the west. Knowing it would be impossible to drag their second beach apparatus to the scene of the wreck due to the tangled masses of telephone, telegraph, and electrical wiring in front of Point Allerton station, Keeper James conferred with his son, Osceola, who agreed to send some of his men back for the Mass Humane Society's Hunt gun at Station #18, on Stony Beach. Osceola hired a team of horses to bring back the equipment, as the rest of the lifesavers headed for the wreck.

Back at the Point Allerton Station, Joshua's wife, Louisa, and the wives of the other surfmen had laid out blankets and hot drinks to care for the survivors of the *Tilton*. Seated in front of a roaring fire in the mess room, the seven sailors finally felt safe for the first time in about 15 hours.

The two crews reached Barge *#1* at about 11 a.m. and set up the Humane Society's beach apparatus. They fired shots with the Hunt gun before realizing that the barge was about to break to pieces. Both keepers, Joshua and Osceola, called for volunteers to wade out into the surf. Tying lines around their waists, a group of surfmen walked out among the wreckage as far as they could, getting as close to the distressed vessel as possible, and trusting their friends on the beach to drag them to safety at the first real sign of danger. Within moments the pilothouse broke off of the barge and rode the waves toward the shore. With a tremendous crash it slammed to earth heavily tossing its passengers into a pile on the beach. The lifesavers in the surf rushed to grab them men before the undertow dragged them back in again. The surfmen held onto the sailors and waited for the next wave to crash, which carried them all to a point on the beach where they could scramble to safety. As the wave hit, though, a flying piece of debris struck the leg of volunteer Louis F Galiano, leaving a deep bone bruise. His heroic rescue work during the Portland Gale ended there and then.

Knowing it would be impossible to bring the survivors back to the station into the driving northeast winds, Joshua looked for the nearest available shelter. He spotted a cottage nearby and banged on the door, but the family had fled. He and his men then crashed down the door, dragging in the helpless forms from the wreck. The crew made a fire, stripped off all of the sailors' wet clothing, and wrapped them in any quilts and blankets they could find. One of the surfmen found the liquor cabinet and heated up some whiskey drinks to warm the survivors from the inside.

As he came to his senses, the master of the barge, Captain Joshua Thomas, started to violently curse the master of the tug, claiming that his crew and the crew of Barge *#4* had been left to die. Apparently, the *#4* had been left at anchor right alongside the *#1*. The Hull lifesavers never even knew it had been there.

Captain Charles Abergh of Barge *#4* had begun desperately blowing his horn to alert a tug shortly after being left to drop anchor off Point Allerton the evening of the 26th. He blew four blasts three times, but received no response. He had to stop when water started coming aboard, reaching the ship's fires. By 11 a.m., she started to drag her anchors into Nantasket Roads.

Joshua James, the venerable keeper of the Point Allerton Life-Saving Station, led the rescues of twenty men from four ships during the storm. United States Coast Guard

When Barge *#4* struck Toddy Rocks about six hours later, three men were lost. The other two, Captain Abergh and his steward, John Vanderveer, clung to life by grabbing on the floating pilothouse, which had broken away from the barge. Miraculously surviving a crash on shore, they scampered along the shoreline to the home of Mr. Amber Cleverly who opened his doors to them. They were warming themselves in front of the fire when the house suddenly titled on its foundation, swaying with the wind. Fearing that the house would collapse, the sailors and the Cleverly family rushed out of the house to the annex of the nearby Pemberton Hotel. Moments after they arrived, the annex filled up with water, and they all had to climb the stairs to the second floor. Later in the day a messenger from the hotel reached the Point Allerton station, and Captain James sent a team to retrieve the stranded seamen and the family. By mid-afternoon the wives of the surfmen were caring for fourteen wet, cold, tired mariners, as well as the Cleverly family.

Finally back at the station in the afternoon, Joshua James spotted a schooner ashore of Great Brewster Island, and knew that there was no way he could launch a boat into such pounding waves. He decided to wait until the surf quieted. As the storm continued to rage, the keeper feared that the night's high tide would be even worse than the morning's, an unbelievable thought, as Hull Village has become a white-capped lake. Down the street, a man could be seen waving his arms frantically through his chamber window, Surfman #1, George F. Pope, Joshua's nephew, launched a dory onto the flooded street and rowed to the man's rescue, bringing him to higher ground.

The storm had spent its fury by the next high tide, around 10:30 p.m., so the lifesavers got a chance to rest. Joshua's men did have to patrol that night, although their keyposts had washed away and the beaches were nearly impassable with wreckage. The next day, though, would be as busy as the first.

At first light the next morning, the Captain used his glass to look out to Boston Light on Little Brewster Island for a predetermined distress signal agreed upon by himself and light keeper Henry Pingree. Seeing it, the U.S.L.S.S. crew and four volunteers launched Massachusetts Humane Society surfboat *#17, Boston Herald* (the only other Humane Society boat built along the same lines as the famous surfboat, *Nantasket*) from Stony Beach and headed for the wreck. Spotting the tug *Ariel*, the Captain arranged to be pulled as close as they could to Great Brewster Island, resting the weary arms of the mixed crew.

An odd sight, this piano, still standing while all around it had blown away, acted as a reminder of the typical mirth of Nantasket Beach in better times. Hull Historical Society

As stated in the local newspaper, Old Boreas had shot the Chutes at Nantasket Beach. Hull Historical Society

When the crew of the tug dared go no further, the surfmen began to row. Passing through a series of breakers, the rescuers finally settled alongside the vessel, the *Calvin F. Baker*, and brought what was left of its crew to safety. Five men had survived to tell their tale. At about 3 a.m. on Sunday they had run ashore on the island. All eight members of the crew were forced to head for the bow as the aft deck crumbled beneath their feet. They climbed the rigging as the ship took on water, and there they remained for approximately thirty hours. Two men, the mate and the second mate, could not hold on during the night and dropped into the water, drowning. A third, the steward, froze to death in place, and when the lifesavers arrived they carried his corpse down into their surfboat, where the master had hot drinks waiting. After being pulled back to Stony Beach, the crew headed back to the station. The five survivors entered the already-overcrowded building and sat down before the fire to thaw out their swollen and frostbitten feet, bringing the total of lucky ones to nineteen. As the crew brought the frozen steward to the morgue, they wondered just how many sailors had not been so unlucky in the past two days.

Stepping back into the lifesaving station around 10:30 a.m., Joshua James received news that yet another coal-carrying vessel had come ashore, this one six miles away on Black Rock, south of Atlantic Hill. Five volunteers joined the station crew as Captain James hired a team of farm horses to pull the Humane Society surfboat *Nantasket* down the peninsula to the wreck.

A Humane Society crew from neighboring Cohasset had attempted to launch directly out to the small island from Stoney Beach, but immediately capsized and retreated to shore, where they found warm blankets and a fire in a nearby home. Three men had seen stranded on the rock flying a signal of distress.

Joshua and his crew decided to launch *Nantasket* from protected Gun Rock Cove, about a mile north of Black Rock, after waiting almost an hour for the seas to abate. They pulled out to the island, rowing with the wind, but had to wait over an hour to make a safe landing. On the island they could see a small gunning hut.

Inside the hut huddled three men, sailors from the coal schooner *Lucy A. Nichols*. The *Nichols* had been released from its tow by the tug *Underwriter* when the storm began, along with the *Virginia*. She had held on admirably for a long time, but finally dragged her anchor and smashed ashore around 9 a.m. Sunday. The captain and the first mate attempted to swim for their lives just before she hit but drowned in the process. In probably the most amazing moment of luck during the entire storm, a mast from the *Nichols* fell directly onto the island, setting up a temporary walkway to safety for the remaining crew. They quickly sprinted across to the island, moments before the vessel completely broke up. They spent the next day and a half inside the small wooden shack.

One man complained of a broken shoulder and showed several contusions about the head and legs. Just before sundown the crew launched *Nantasket* once again, rowing for a mile headlong into a heavy NNW wind. Once on shore, Joshua James hired a team to go on ahead and call for a doctor to meet them at the station. At 7 p.m., the crew finally returned to the station for the night.

Observing the damage on the way home, Keeper James saw downed wiring all over town. Hotels had simply vanished, and wreckage from buildings and ships littered the shore. All along the beach laid thousands and thousands of tons of coal.

Back at the Point Allerton station, 22 survivors from five different vessels found comfort thanks to the tireless efforts of the women of the town, a different breed of lifesaver, but altogether as important. Bodies of drowned sailors had begun to wash ashore, and the town's "dead house" filled up quickly. News soon arrived that the steamer *Portland* had disappeared off of Race Point, and that 160 people were feared dead, more than had died on the entire Massachusetts coast in the Great Storm of 1888. For Joshua James, the year 1898 had been the most destructive he had ever lived through, and there was still a month to go.

THE LIFESAVERS
David Atkins, Hero of Cape Cod
by Donna Hill (Volume 2, Number 4)

DURING the first seven years of his service as keeper of the Peaked Hill Bars Life-Saving Station, David Atkins proved again and again that he was a dedicated and courageous lifesaver. In the end, he considered himself a disgrace.

Captain Atkins had been appointed when Peaked Hill Bars was first established in 1872, one of the original nine stations of the United States Life-Saving Service on Cape Cod. Atkins' station was two and a half miles east of Provincetown, Massachusetts, on a coast where hidden rips, cross currents and two rows of shifting sand bars caused so many disasters that the coast became known as the Ocean Graveyard.

Surfmen from Peaked Hill Bars Station patrolled west about half way to meet the surfmen from Race Point Life-Saving Station on the tip of the Cape, and east to meet surfmen from Highland USLSS Station. At that time, surfmen from those three stations covered the northern stretch of the Cape.

In spite of their vigilance and great valor, surfmen were not always able to save lives of those shipwrecked on that perilous coast. Sometimes they even lost their own. Such was the case in three disastrous wrecks at Peaked Hill Bars.

Two of these wrecks directly and one indirectly, involved the use of three different guns designed to shoot a line to stranded vessels so that the breeches buoy could be hauled out to rescue survivors one at a time when surfboats could not be launched.

One such instance occurred on March 4, 1875, during a terrible storm in which the Italian bark *Giovanni* foundered off Peaked Hill Bars. The gun the lifesavers relied upon to shoot a line to the *Giovanni* was an unwieldy cast-iron mortar with a range of only 421 yards, not far enough to reach the wreck. The lifesavers could only stand by in horror as all fourteen lives on that vessel were lost.

In the hope of preventing another such tragedy officers of the Ordnance Corps prompted efforts to increase the range of the lifesavers' artillery. R.P. Parrott of West Point Foundry designed several new guns, one of which had a range of 631 yards, although it was too heavy to be easily transported. The gun was delivered to the Peaked Hill Bars Life-Saving Station during the fiscal year 1875-76, following that of the wreck of the *Giovanni.*

Although the Parrott gun was better than its predecessor, greater portability and range were still needed. During fiscal 1877-78, in what the Life-Saving Service called the most remarkable achievement of the year, Lieutenant David A. Lyle of the Ordnance Department, U.S. Army, perfected a bronze, rust-proof gun weighing only 185 pounds easily carried by two men. With a range of 695 yards, the Lyle gun could reach most vessels wrecked on the Cape. It used a shot line made of braided, bleached linen thread, waterproof, and elastic enough to help prevent breaking. The eye of the shot protruded four inches from the gun's muzzle, thus keeping the shot line from being burned off by gasses ignited in firing.

The Lyle gun was delivered to Peaked Hill Bars Life-Saving Station but not soon enough for Captain Atkins to become familiar with it before another wreck occurred within his jurisdiction.

April 4, 1879, about one-thirty a.m. on a dark, snowy night, the three-masted schooner *Sarah J. Fort* from Tuckerton, New Jersey, bound from Hoboken, New Jersey, for Boston with a cargo of coal, foundered off Peaked Hill Bars Life-Saving Station, about a quarter of a mile from shore.

The stranded schooner could not at first be seen by the surfman patrolling the beach. Later some bits of wreckage were found but were assumed to be from a vessel that had sunk elsewhere several days before. Not until three a.m. could a dim outline of the schooner be seen through the storm.

Keeper Atkins ordered out the crew. The men struggled nearly two miles along the beach through snow, wind and heavy, slushy sand but could not get their surfboat to the scene until daybreak, about four-thirty.

Not long afterwards, Keeper (often called Captain) John W. Young from Race Point Life-Saving Station and Keeper Edwin P. Worthen from Highland Life-Saving Station appeared with some of their surfmen and offered to help.

By then the sea was rushing over the hull of the schooner and it was already a ruin, her main and mizzenmasts unstepped and wavering, her frame

Peaked Hill Bars Life-Saving Station on Cape Cod, Massachusetts. This was the 1872-73 red house-type station where Keeper David Atkins and his crew served.
William Quinn

disintegrating and her wreckage bounding on the waves between ship and shore. Her six crewmen were in the forerigging, hanging on desperately.

In such a storm, with high tide, violent sea and surf, the men could not get their surfboat out. They had to rely on the breeches buoy to bring back the unfortunate seamen. Atkins chose the Parrott gun with which he was familiar, and which, because it was larger and heavier than the new Lyle gun, he judged to have greater power. He went back to the station for some of his crew to help bring the Parrott gun to the scene in a hand barrel.

With the Parrott gun and breeches buoy equipment finally in position, Atkins and his crew struggled for hours, firing nine times in an effort to reach the wreck. But they had to aim into the eye of the storm, and the line shot by the Parrott gun either fell short or was burned off by the increased charges of powder that the surfmen used in a frantic effort to extend the range of their cannon.

About seven o'clock, the schooner's main and mizzenmasts fell. Later the foremast fell, but its rigging remained attached to the schooner, allowing the mast to plunge wildly in the sea round the hull. About ten o'clock, while the struggling lifesavers looked on in anguish, the ship's cook and mate fell out of the rigging and were swept away in the sea.

By eleven a.m., when the tide began to ebb, the four remaining seamen were able to leave the rigging and take refuge in the port bow, the only part of the schooner that was not yet submerged.

The surfmen went on firing their Parrott gun without success until noon. At low tide it became possible to launch the surfboat. In the first attempt, the boat was swamped. The surfmen bailed it out and tried again, but the boat was slammed back on the beach and its ribs broken.

A crowd of people had gathered from Provincetown. A whaleboat, although smaller than was expected, was brought to the scene as a substitute. Among the crowd was Captain Isaac F. Mayo, an experienced and courageous lifesaver, who took command of the whaleboat.

Although frost-bitten from exposure in freezing weather and exhausted from hours of labor without having had anything to eat since the day before, Atkins and his men pleased to go out again. However, Captain Mayo wisely chose a fresh crew from other men present.

The whaleboat, too, was swamped on the first try to launch; but on the second, although half full of water, the boat got past the breakers, where the crew bailed it out, rowed on and reached the schooner. They found the four stranded seamen nearly helpless and had to lift them into the boat one at a time.

The most hazardous part of the rescue lay ahead. The small, overcrowded boat had to plunge through rough seas among thrashing timbers, snarled cordage and canvas from the wreck.

As the boat neared shore, a great wave overtook it and threw it end over end, casting everyone into the raging surf and undertow. Fortunately, the townspeople did not hesitate to rush out into the surf to rescue the victims, some of whom were trapped under the boat.

The shipwreck survivors were nearly unconscious. They and surfmen alike were suffering from exhaustion, exposure and frostbite. All were taken to the Peaked Hill Bars Life-Saving Station, given restoratives from the station medicine chest, and put into warm blankets.

Food had been prepared by Mrs. Mayo and Mrs. Atkins, who had walked out from Provincetown through the storm to offer help in whatever way they could, including care of frostbitten hands. A physician, a Dr. Crocker, was called.

In the official investigation that followed, Captain Mayo was awarded a gold medal for heroism. Captain Atkins was commended for his courageous efforts and pronounced blameless in the tragic loss of life, but it was acknowledged that if he had used the Lyle gun instead of the Parrott, his surfmen could have reached the wreck of the *Sara J. Fort* with the breeches buoy and very likely have saved the whole crew. Even though the authorities exonerated Atkins and sustained him in his post as keeper of the station, Atkins himself felt terrible guilt. Townspeople subjected him and his crew to what was called the "goading slur."

Atkins and his crew bore the sneers and jeers meekly but at the start of the following season, when Atkins left his home in Provincetown, he is said to have told his wife that before the season was over, he would wipe out the "goading slur." He would die at his post rather than disgrace himself or the Life-Saving Service again.

And so he did, November 30, 1880, in a heroic rescue effort at the wreck of the sloop *C.E. Trumbull*. As was so often said of the surfmen, they felt they had to go out, but they did not have to come back. In this instance, Atkins and two of his surfmen, Elisha M. Taylor and Stephen F. Mayo, did not come back, and neither did two of the seamen they tried to rescue, the captain and a pilot, but for very different reasons.

About 4 a.m. on November 30, the sloop *C.E. Trumbull* of Rockport, Massachusetts, bound for home from New Bedford with twenty tons of coal for ballast, was stranded on the outer bars off Peaked Hill Bars Life-Saving Station in a violent northwest wind.

Leaving one surfman, John L. Cole, ashore to keep lanterns burning, Atkins and five others of his crew rowed out to the vessel. They went up on the lee quarter of the endangered ship and tossed a line to the seamen, who made it fast aboard. Keeper Atkins called to the men to get in the surfboat. Four of them complied but the captain and the pilot refused, saying they wanted to collect their belongings. With that, Atkins told them to cast off. When they would not, he ordered the line cut. He and his crew took the four men safely to shore to be cared for at their stations.

Atkins and his crew went out again for the sloop's captain and the pilot. By then the sloop was rolling, the boom slapping the sea. The boom caught the surfboat under its cork belt and threw it over, bottom up. The surfmen turned the boat right side up, but it would not stay. They tried again, but the boat turned over and threw the men out. Three of the surfmen, Charles P. Kelly, Samuel O. Fisher and Isaiah H. Young, struck out for shore, but Atkins, Elisha M. Taylor and Stephen F. Mayo clung to the boat.

Surfman John Cole, on shore, with the lanterns, found Kelly exhausted on the beach. Kelly said, "They are all lost." Later Cole found Fisher, who was without boots, hat or coat. He found Young just barely clear of the surf and nearly senseless.

Keeper Atkins and the two surfmen who had stayed with the surfboat did not make it to shore alive. The keeper of Highland Life-Saving Station, Captain Edwin P. Worthen, and his crew discovered the bodies.

On the morning of the disaster, Highland Surfman L.B. Small, on patrol to the north, saw something dark rolling in the surf. At first he thought it was seaweed, but then he realized that it was a man. When he pulled the man ashore, he was horrified to see from the cork life belt the man was wearing that he was a USLSS lifesaver. Small thought he recognized Captain Atkins from their neighboring station. Small tried in vain to revive him. Finally, he took him farther up the beach and covered his grave with his life belt.

Rushing back to Highland station to report to his keeper, Small saw another body sweeping alongshore in an undertow, beyond reach.

The second Peaked Hill Bars Life-Saving Station was this Isles of Shoals-type station. Note the encroaching sea. The station was later moved inland. Sadly, only its foundation remains today. William Quinn

Keeper Worthen and Surfman Anton T. Lucas ran to the scene. Seeing the man in the undertow, Worthen threw off his coat and mittens, dashed out and was nearly swept away himself before he managed to reach the body and bring it ashore. It proved to be that of Elisha Taylor. He too was beyond restoration.

Then Worthen saw Stephen Mayo pulled along in the surf, supported by his life belt, his face held up and recognizable, but he was swept away.

Wet and freezing, Worthen left Lucas with the bodies and returned to Highland station to change his clothes and to send men out with grapnel and a line to try to recover Mayo's body.

Worthen asked a member of his crew, young Atkins, the son of Captain Atkins, to come along while he went to telegraph the USLSS district superintendent, Benjamin C. Sparrow. On the way, Keeper Worthen told the young surfman, Atkins, the tragic news about his father, and sent him home to his mother.

Worthen went back to the scene and helped to recover Mayo's body.

Another account of finding the bodies of Atkins, Taylor and Mayo is given by a Katherine Crosby, supposedly by a surfman from Highland station. Told many years after the event and inaccurate in some details, it is nevertheless a moving account of the anguish the men from Highland Station felt. Dead bodies were nothing new to them, but the surfmen stood dumbstruck, heads bare in the gray morning, breakers thundering behind them as they stared down at the remains of Keeper Atkins, a fellow lifesaver they had long admired.

The funerals of the deceased surfmen were held on a bright winter day, December 3, at the Centre Methodist Episcopal church in Provincetown. Captain Atkins had wiped out the goading slur, and the whole Cape was in mourning. Business was suspended. Flags on all stations of the Life-Saving Service were at half-mast, as were those on the wharves and vessels in the harbor. The fire department turned out in full. At least fifteen hundred people crowded the church, and many more, unable to get in, waited outside.

Surfmen from neighboring stations bore the coffins, which were covered with flowers. When the wounded survivors of Peaked Hill Bars station bent over the coffins of their fallen comrades to say goodbye, the whole congregation sobbed.

At the time of his death, Keeper David H. Atkins was forty-six years old. Previous to his appointment as keeper of Peaked Hill Bars station, he had worked as a whaler and a fisherman.

Another tragic aspect of the death of surfmen during the early days was that they often left dependents nearly destitute. Keeper Atkins left his widow and two children with almost nothing. Surfman Taylor also left a widow and several small children. Surfman Mayo was not married, but he was the only child and support of elderly parents, his father in poor health. Of the surviving surfmen, Kelly and Fisher recovered, but Surfman Young sustained chest pain, hemorrhaging in his lungs, and one leg paralyzed. He never regained his health.

Outraged that there was neither compensation for the dependents of surfmen who were killed, nor for injured surfmen, citizens raised a subscription statewide. Unofficial report was that Atkins' family received eleven hundred dollars, the equivalent at that time of only two years, nine months of a keeper's salary. The others also received meager compensation, although welcome, no doubt, and unexpected.

Ironically the captain and pilot who had remained aboard the *C.E. Trumbull*, and the sloop itself, fared well.

Immediately after the surfboat capsized, the vessel slipped off the bar and drifted away with the captain and pilot aboard. About nine a.m. that morning, the sloop was seen wallowing in the surf at Chatham, colors flying for help. A wrecking crew went aboard, provided a jib and three new crewmen and took the *C.E. Trumbull* on course for Boston.

THE LIFESAVERS
·· · ·· — ·· · ··   ·· · ·· — ·· · ··   ·· · ·· — ·· · ··

Robert M. Small: The Training of a Life-Saving Service Keeper
by Frederick Stonehouse (Volume 4, Number 2)

THE men who manned the sweep oar in the old Life-Saving Service were a breed unto themselves. Outstanding seamen, they were utterly fearless in the face of the most dreadful danger. Regardless of the situation, they always would launch their boats and steer for those in distress.

Robert. M. Small was a fine example of such a keeper. Born at Kincardine, Ontario, on the shore of Lake Huron on December 9, 1862, from age 12 he spent his time on the lakes fishing and sailing. At age 15 he left home and found work with commercial fisherman at East Tawas, Michigan, also on Lake Huron. The work was hard and the hours long. The fish boats were out in every kind of weather, fair and foul. It was as a commercial fisherman Small honed his skills handling small boats under both sail and oar. Considering that he was one of 14 brothers and sisters, he was likely anxious to make his own way in the world. During the winter months, when the lake froze, preventing fishing, he went to formal school and in his spare time, put up ice. Harvesting ice was big business at Tawas Bay. Crews of up to 300 men worked to load and ship thousands of rail cars filled with ice to Detroit, Chicago and Cleveland markets. Of course, some of the ice went into local ice houses for use in shipping dairy products and fish. The heavy physical labor of fishing and working the ice produced a very strong young man, ready to tackle life's challenges head on. By age 18 he had gained U.S. citizenship.

In the spring of 1881, at age 18, he applied for a position as surfman at the Ottawa Point Life-Saving Station, now known as Tawas Point. Legendary keeper George W. Plough must have liked the cut of the youngster because he accepted him into his veteran crew. Plough was the keeper who led his crew on the desperate rescue of the *St. Clair* sailors on October 1, 1888.

His time spent at Ottawa Point was not exciting, but it was a good opportunity to learn his new profession. For a young lifesaver his first turn-out was probably exciting enough, exactly what would turn a young man's head. At 2:00 p.m. on July 12, 1881, the patrol discovered a small schooner ashore on Ottawa Point, half a mile from the station. The men quickly launched the surfboat and rowed over to the vessel, which turned out to be the *Nakick* of Bay City, Michigan. She was bound from East Tawas to Au Gres when the accident happened. Aboard was an excursion party of 13 persons, including six young women. After two hours of work the lifesavers were able to free the schooner and send her on her way to the great thanks of all aboard, especially the women. It was a great way to break up a young lifesaver's routine.

On September 19, the patrol was able to warn off a steamer with a Coston signal that was heading for the beach. Two months later the crew was busy trying to free the tug *W.E. Quinby* which had grounded in the bay while working to recover some logging chains. After two hours of work they had her off the bottom.

Small remained at Ottawa Point for three years, learning the many tricks of the lifesaver's trade. In the spring of 1884, he transferred to the Point Au Barques Station, 50 miles down the Lake Huron coast on Michigan's thumb. The area was a notorious ship trap with over 70 vessels wrecked in the vicinity. He remained there for six years under the command of keeper Harry D. Ferris. Small must have kept up with the folks back in Kincardine because on December 23, 1885, he married Rebecca Maud Bennett, a girl from Kincardine. The ceremony was performed in the city that was home to both.

While at Port Au Barques, Small participated in a number of dangerous rescues. The first of them, the *Mona*, illustrates the frustration the crews sometimes encountered in trying to do their job. At 1:00 a.m. on September 10, 1887, the scow schooner *Mona* was sailing downbound in a gale off Point Au Barques with a full cargo of lumber when she started to leak.

Waterlogged and unmanageable, she drifted ashore two miles south of the station. The patrol spotted her immediately and burned a Coston signal but got no response from the schooner. Since the sails were furled and she was laying head to wind, the surfman thought she was in no immediate danger. Nonetheless, he reported it at once to the keeper. When Ferris examined it with his glass he thought she was anchored outside the reef. He directed a close watch be kept on her. At 6:00 a.m. the lookout thought he saw a distress

Tawas Life-Saving Station's surfmen circa 1905. Keeper R.M. Small is at the steering oar on Lake Huron. Richard Small

signal so the crew launched the big lifeboat and rowed out to the vessel. It was a tough row, with a difficult trip through the stormy surf. When they were about two thirds of the way to the vessel, the schooner's crew, unable to see the lifesavers approaching from windward, took to a makeshift raft and headed for the beach, landing five minutes before the lifesavers reached the *Mona*. Finding the schooner deserted, the keeper landed his men on the beach opposite the vessel where they discovered the crew, consisting of a captain, three sailors and woman cook. All were drenched and exhausted. The keeper sent for a horse and buggy and dispatched the woman to the station on it, while the others proceeded on foot. All were given supplies from the Woman's National Relief Association stocks. The captain of the *Mona* said he had seen the Coston signal but since his matches were wet, could not reply to it. At daybreak he hoisted his oilskin coat on the mast halyard which was the signal the lookout finally saw. While the sailors were sent south to Sand Beach, the lifesavers went to work stripping out the schooner. On September 23, she went to pieces during a gale, becoming a total loss.

The next month Small was in the middle of another rescue. At 2:00 a.m. on October 3, the steamer *Albion* was towing the schooner *Ark* when both went on the rocks about a mile and a quarter northeast of Grindstone City, Michigan. The night was very dark and lashed by heavy rain but the Grindstone City patrol spotted the vessels within ten minutes of striking. As he was hurrying back to the station he ran into some of the steamer's crew who had rowed ashore in the yawl to find out where they were. Alerted by the patrol, keeper Henry Gill ordered out the surfboat and went out to the vessel. The captain asked him to wire for tugs and to bring the ship's female cook and boy ashore just in case. The lifesavers returned to the station with the pair but when a strong gale blew up from the west, returned to the *Albion* and removed the remaining ten men of the crew. When the gale blew itself out several days later, the steamer was a total loss. The pounding breakers had reduced her to kindling!

The schooner *Ark*, somewhat to the east of the steamer, was also in trouble. At daybreak she flew a distress signal asking for her crew to be taken off. The Grindstone City crew responded but ended up with the steamer crew instead. The crew from Point Au Barques Station, seven miles to the southeast, also saw the signal and launched their lifeboat in response. It was a long difficult pull against the westerly seas and doubtlessly Small learned something of the stamina needed to be a successful surfman. Finally reaching the schooner, they took the ten man crew aboard and brought them to the city dock. Turning the heavy lifeboat around, they rowed back to their own station. On the afternoon of the October 8, the crew rowed back to the schooner again and helped a local tug recover her.

Small's worst storm experience on the lower lakes was likely during the *A. Booty* wreck on November 11, 1887. The schooner went ashore on Port Austin Reef, about three miles from the Grindstone City Station at 1:00 a.m., during a terrific north storm. The patrol soon discovered her and brought the alarm back to the Grindstone Station. The lifesavers set out with their surfboat in a wagon, reaching the beach opposite the wreck at 5:00 a.m. By the grey light of the cold dawn it was apparent that the storm was far too rough for the light surfboat. The keeper sent part of the crew back to the station with the wagon and team to get the beach apparatus. When they returned with it, their shots fell short, even with the highest powder charges. The wreck was too far out. Never giving up, the keeper thought if he could launch the big lifeboat to the westward of the wreck, the storm would blow him down on it and he could reach her. But he had no wagon strong enough for the heavy boat.

Keeper Gill telegraphed to keeper Ferris at Point Au Barques at 1:00 p.m., asking him to bring his lifeboat and crew to the wreck site. His boat was somewhat lighter than the big English lifeboat Grindstone City had. Extremely seaworthy, their only drawback was their weight, an estimated 4,000 pounds. The Point Au Barques boat was a Dobbins boat. Developed by the superintendent of the Ninth District, it was self-ballasting and weighed between 1,600 - 2,000 pounds, thus it could be more easily man-handled into the beach. By 4:00 p.m., however, a wagon big enough to haul the big Grindstone City boat was found and the crew were on their way to the beach with it.

The Point Au Barques crew had already arrived at the scene with their lifeboat and assisted by the bystanders, bravely launched into the thundering surf. In Keeper Ferris' words, "...made good headway until about 200 yards from wreck found a terrible strong current which was running down the shore from the westward being a (unintelligible) to wind and breakers drifted boat to leeward of wreck in spite of all efforts of self and crew, wreck being hard on reef and sea splitting, the breakers which could run from two different directions. One terrible breaker striking my port bow, the next my starboard bow, driving boat before it like lightning. My steering oar was torn from my hands and snatched out of the steering lock. No. 1 saving me from being thrown overboard by catching my foot. No. 1 relayed my orders to crew who kept boat headed up until keeper (released) lashings of a spare oar which was

Tawas Point Life-Saving Station on Lake Huron circa 1905. Keeper R.M. Small is in the dark suit at the bottom. Richard Small

used for a steering oar." The current proved too strong for them and they were blown leeward and buffeted badly by the cross chop. The sight of the lone lifeboat battling the seas was a magnificent one. At times the huge waves nearly stood the lifeboat on end! Keeper Ferris expertly guided his boat to a safe landing on a small sand beach. Not beaten yet, the lifesavers brought the boat back to the original launching location for another try. By now it was dark and nothing of the schooner could be seen from the beach. The blackness was accented by the loud roaring of the waves. Again they launched into the crashing surf. Now Ferris steered westward in an effort to come down on the vessel with the waves. For two long hours the lifesavers strained at their long oars. Finally they sighted a faint yellow light streaming out the schooners cabin windows. At least they knew where she was. Just when they were certain they would reach her, the boat was grabbed by a powerful current and swept away into a rapids of reef born breakers. Again they were driven to the wreck's lee. And again they rowed for all they were worth, forcing fatigued muscles to keep the oars biting deep into the rolling lake. After half an hour they knew they had failed. No progress toward the schooner was being made. Reluctantly, facing the obvious, Ferris brought his men back to the beach. The men were utterly exhausted, beaten by the lake, at least for the moment. The crew went up to the lighthouse where the light keeper's wife gave them hot coffee and food.

Meanwhile the Grindstone City crew had arrived with their big lifeboat shortly after the Point Au Barques men made their second try. After the two keepers talked the matter over, it was decided that no further attempts would be made until after first light. At dawn the Grindstone boat was launched, manned by both crews, a total of 14 men at the oars! They would not want for muscle power! Smashing its way through the waves, the lifeboat soon slid neatly under the schooner's jib-boom and the crew of six men and one woman tumbled aboard. Within minutes they were all safe on the beach. From this rescue Small certainly learned the value of teamwork, not only within one crew but also with other crews. What one crew could not do, two could! He also gained the invaluable experience of using both the Dobbins boat and English boats and something of the punishment the boats could endure. The Dobbins boat had been damaged in the earlier *Mona* rescue and during the *A. Booty* rescue had started to open her seams.

His experience and leadership must have been evident to all because on March 9, 1890, he was appointed keeper at Crisp Point Station on far-off Lake Superior. This station was one of four built in 1876 along the lake's infamous "Shipwreck Coast." Stretching west from Whitefish Point and about eight miles apart, they are Vermillion Point, Crisp Point, Two-Hearted River and Deer Park. All of the stations were very isolated, with no civilization for many miles. Small and his wife made the best they could of their lonely and desolate posting. During the harsh winters, his wife returned to Kincardine to be with both families.

Some mariners said there was a shipwreck for every mile of this treacherous coast. Small certainly had his opportunities to pluck sailors from certain death. One wreck was particularly devastating. On May 3, 1891, the steamer *Wilhelm* was upbound for Duluth towing the schooner *Atlanta*. About 35 miles to the northwest of Whitefish Point, the wind shifted northwest and a severe gale set in. This happened around 7:00 p.m. The *Wilhelm* continued on until 11:00 p.m., when the storm grew too powerful to keep battering into and she turned back for shelter behind Whitefish Point. While making the turn the tow line to the *Atlanta* snapped. Unable to reconnect in the wild lake storm, the steamer left the schooner to her fate and continued back to shelter at Whitefish Point. The crew on the *Atlanta* hoisted sail in an effort to follow the steamer but the powerful blasts of wind snapped the foreboom in two and blew the sails into flapping ribbons of canvas. For twenty minutes she ran hard before the storm driven by bare poles before she broached. Wallowing side to side in the heaving waves she sprang a plank and started to quickly fill with water. Waves swept over her deck. The crew worked desperately at the pumps but could not gain on the flood entering her hold. When Captain James L. Knowlton sounded her hold at 11:00 a.m. the next day he found ten feet of water! Since the screaming northwester gave no sign of blowing itself out, the captain ordered the crew of seven, including a woman cook, to abandon her in the yawl. Ten minutes after they pulled away from the schooner she dove for the bottom. At this point they were about twenty miles off the shipwreck coast.

Captain Knowlton kept the small boat's head to the crashing seas as it drifted quickly to leeward. About 5:00 p.m. the survivors spotted the gray line of the Michigan shore in the vicinity of Crisp Point. The waves were building as they approached the shoal water inshore and the resulting surf was tremendous. Some of the crew later said Knowlton wanted to keep going down the coast to the east where they could safely land behind Whitefish Point. His crew though, was worn out from their struggle and strength sapped by the exposure in the yawl. They insisted on trying to land near the life-saving station. At this point one of the men crabbed his oar and was tossed out of the boat. While pulling him back aboard, the boat swung off before the

Ottawa Point (Tawas) Life-Saving Station crew, circa 1882. The name was changed to Tawas Point in 1903. R.M. Small is a crew member, Keeper George W. Plough is at the sweep. Richard Small

wind. Now there was no choice. They had to run for the beach. When they came into the outer breakers, the small yawl, never designed for such conditions, nearly pitch-poled and three men, including the captain, mate and a sailor were thrown into the boiling surf and drowned. Stiff from the long exposure, they were unable to help themselves. After bobbing in the waves once or twice, they sank in the dark, boiling water and were gone. Meanwhile the yawl had swung broadside to the waves and the next sea rolled her over, dumping the remaining four people into the water. Another wave turned the boat right side up and the survivors clung desperately to the gunwale. Another crashing billow turned the boat over again, sweeping the cook and another sailor to their doom. At this point the lifesavers rushed into the surf and pulled the two remaining sailors, Eli Wait and John Pickel to safety.

Small and his men had not been idle during the wreck, but there was some confusion as to what was happening. In the midst of a Superior norther it is tough to see clearly for any distance and this added to the difficulty. The station lookout had sighted the boat some distance out but identified it as a log or tree root. Both were commonly seen during storms. He paid no more attention to it. Looking directly into a stinging norther was hard enough, without watching trees floating around! The township supervisor, William

Hawkin, was walking along the beach and spotted the boat as it entered the breakers. At first he thought it was the station boat out for a drill. He quickly realized his error and gave the alarm. Small immediately ordered the lifeboat launched, but by the time they started it moving down the rails the yawl was directly in the breakers, about 50 yards west from shore and 75 yards down the beach to the east and drifting very fast. Grabbing life preservers and rope, Small and his men ran after it. By the time they caught up with it, they were only able to reach the two sailors. Small himself ran out into the breakers and managed to bring one of them to the beach. The man was unconscious and nearly dead. Surfman McKenzie was able to rescue another in the same condition. Other lifesavers, rigged with jackets and safety lines, tried to reach the rest but were unable to do so. Surfman Stewart was able to grab the bed quilt that the woman was wrapped in, however she slipped out and sank in the undertow. Other surfmen worked over the near lifeless bodies of the two sailors. It took two hours of effort before the sailors came around. The body of the captain was found on May 22, twelve miles to the east. Surfman McKanna, the lookout that failed to see the yawl when it was nearly ashore, was promptly discharged by Small.

A powerful lake storm on the end of September, 1895, battered Superior shipping. High seas on the 26th sent the steamer *Montana* into the Portage Lake Ship Canal where she smashed into a submerged object and sank to the bottom. On the 28th the schooner-barge *Elma* crashed into towering sandstone cliffs of Miner's Castle at the Pictured Rocks, becoming a total loss. The next day the big steamer *Charles J. Kershaw* with her consorts the *Moonlight* and *Henry A. Kent* were driven ashore just east of Marquette. Keeper Henry Cleary and his Marquette crew performed one of the most spectacular rescues ever performed on the lakes when they plucked the steamer's crew off the rapidly disintegrating vessel.

Small and his Crisp Point crew had their share in the destruction. At 7:30 a.m. Small received a telephone call from the Vermilion keeper that there was a schooner in trouble to the east. Small and his men immediately launched their big lifeboat but after an hour of effort, were unable to cross the outer bar in the crashing waves. They tried again at 10:30 a.m. and succeeded. Four hours later they reached the schooner *Chester B. Jones*, anchored about a mile offshore with a cargo of lumber. Small and his men stood by her until dark, when with the wind and waves continuing to increase, the captain asked to have his crew taken off. He was certain the ship would come apart in the now breaking seas. Small loaded them all into the lifeboat and headed for

Vermilion, the nearest station. It was a long, tough row. About four or five hundred yards off shore, a rogue wave reared up out of the black storm and capsized the boat, throwing all 15 hands into the frigid water. Small's well trained crew were able to right the boat and somehow managed to get everyone back aboard. About 8:00 p.m. the keeper brought the boat safely to the beach at Vermilion.

In the spring of 1897, he was transferred to Ottawa Point Station where he entered the service, replacing keeper Frank J. Ocha who had "disappeared" in October of the previous year. While keeper at Tawas, he didn't live at the station but rented a house in town so his family could enjoy some of the advantages of civilization. After Crisp Point they deserved at least that much. He used a horse and buckboard to commute from the house to the station. Although the road to the station was rough, it was better than trying to row across the bay. He also took advantage of old his fishing employer to obtain a small pond net he set in front of the station. This assured fresh lake trout, herring and perch for his crew. Considering that his men were paying for meals as did surfman all over the service, this did help to cut down on their expenses.

Small and his wife had six children. Two daughters died at birth. Of the four sons, three ended up joining the Coast Guard! The fourth was blind in one eye and unable to pass the physical.

Small remained at Tawas for 17 years, finally retiring on July 1, 1915, after 34 years of service. Like many of the old keepers, he had held out for the retirement pension made possible by combining the Revenue Marine and Life-Savers into the new Coast Guard. He moved into town and enjoyed living with his family full time.

Small's retirement dinner was held at the prestigious Holland Hotel in Tawas. People came from far and wide. In attendance were the mayor and city council, county supervisors, members of the Tawas Beach Club (this club was very exclusive, made up of wealthy people from the Detroit area who summered in Tawas), all the local commercial fishermen, church leaders and of course, his old life-saving friends. After the dinner the men were given cigars and large snifters of brandy. Then the speeches were given, all testifying to Small's courage and accomplishments during his long career.

After retirement, Small still occasionally visited at the station with his good friend keeper James A. Carpenter who replaced him. In at least one instance, Small was back in the surfboat and heading out for a rescue just like in the old days! It seems that a John North, a very experienced Tawas sailor was hired by the wealthy owner of a Detroit sailing yacht to bring her up to the city for the summer. The crew was made up of North, the owner and his son. All went well until they were entering Tawas Bay when a strong southwest wind blew up. The owner and his son panicked and were useless in handling any of the sails. The surfman in the watch tower saw the boat was in danger of foundering and alerted Carpenter. The keeper promptly called out the surfboat. Before they left the dock, he loaded Small and another man into the boat. When the lifesavers reached the beleaguered craft, Small and his companion scampered aboard and helped North sail her safely to a slip at the Tawas Beach Club. It seems even old-timers could still lend a hand once in a while!

Robert M. Small "crossed the bar," as old lake sailors said, in 1935. He was certainly among the last of a rare breed of men, the "Storm Warriors," of the Great Lakes.

THE LIFESAVERS

Surfman William Drazel of the Louisville Floating Life-Saving Station

by John J. Galluzzo (Volume 4, Number 2)

"**SOME** things have happened around here," Surfman William Drazel told the *Louisville Courier Journal* in May of 1921, "that make me believe the day of miracles hasn't passed." If anybody would know about miracles on the Ohio River, it would be Drazel, who spent 40 years as a member of the crew of the floating Louisville, Kentucky U.S. Life-Saving (and later U.S. Coast Guard) Station. What he neglected to mention was that many of the miraculous lifesaving rescues on the river could never have been enacted without his skilled oarsmanship, dedication to the preservation of human life and "semper paratus" vigilance.

William Drazel first joined the crew of the Louisville floating life-saving station as a young man of 20 on April 1, 1882, just four months after the establishment of the station in December, 1881. Although he never kept accurate records, he estimated that over the course of the next four decades he responded to approximately 2,000 distress calls, aided between 5,000 and 7,000 endangered persons, assisted in saving $6,000,000 - $7,000,000 worth of property, and pulled 400 dead bodies from the depths of the Ohio River.

The rapids of the Ohio afforded many life-saving opportunities to local boatmen. Vessels traveling upstream could pass safely through a system of locks, bypassing the dam at the Falls of the Ohio. Yet negotiating a vessel downstream caused headaches for steamboat captains and flatboat fishermen alike, as the only passage was through two fast-moving chutes. Three local rivermen – William Devan, John Gilgooly, and John Tully – saved 45 people from drowning as volunteers between 1875 and 1881, and had each earned a

The only Government
Inland Life Saving Station
in the United States,
Louisville, Ky.

Louisville floating Life-Saving Station with life-skiff (pulling rescue boat) and surfmen. Louisville was the only USLSS station not on either seacoast or lakeshore and it was a busy station indeed. Shown here is the second vessel used as a life-saving station at Louisville, Kentucky, built in 1903. Shanks Collection

gold medal from the USLSS. When the Louisville station opened in 1881, all three joined the crew.

Even more dangerous than the rapids, though, were the periodic horrendous floods, caused by torrential rains that swelled the river until it overflowed its banks and swallowed up everything for miles, submerging many houses, and driving other residents up onto their roofs where they could expect to sit for days without sustenance, until the waters receded.

For precisely these two reasons, the USLSS built their first, innovative floating station in 1881, positioned usually just above the dam, but capable of being towed to the spot of an emergency whenever necessary. A fixed station would have been of no use whatsoever during a typical Ohio River flood, since the river level greatly fluctuates and the banks overflow.

The first station consisted of a two-story riverboat-like structure set on a scow-shaped hull, and topped with the ever-present Life-Saving Service lookout tower. The surfmen, who retained the same title as their coastal life-saving brethren, yet who knew nothing about the actions of the surf, served year round from the time of the station's establishment, due to the dangerous nature of the Falls. They manned two low, fast skiffs, boats unlike any other in the service, known as *Reckless* and *Ready*. The first Louisville station remained in service until November of 1902, when it was replaced by a newer, more modern station. The Coast Guard replaced that station in 1929 with a third floating station.

Louisville's first keeper, Captain "Billy" Devan, served until his death in 1911. Surfman John Gillooly, with more than 28 years in service, took over at that point, continuing as keeper until retiring in 1916. After Gillooly retired, the Coast Guard transferred in two successive warrant officers from the Great Lakes, who, although given proper respect by their men, were never seen as true "rivermen." Surfman Drazel, although he outlasted all of the members of the original crew, never reached the level of keeper.

Throughout the course of his Life-Saving Service and Coast Guard career, Drazel fought through floods, ice floes, and raging rapids to help those in need. In 1891, after a severe tornado tore through the Louisville area, he and other members of the crew cruised the river searching for wreckage. Through blinding rain he caught sight of the endangered steamer *Hibernia*, headed for the falls. The boat raced through some rapids, with the lifesavers in chase, before safely coming to halt near the Louisville Bridge. They succeeded in saving all fourteen people aboard.

Drazel's watchful eye caught first sight of a number of endangered steamships over the years from the station's tower, that for one reason or another found themselves on a collision course with the dam, including *Monterey*, *Lena May*, *Buckeye State*, and *Queen City*.

On February 10, 1914, the steamer *Queen City* left Pittsburgh bound for the Mardi Gras celebration in New Orleans, planning to ride the Ohio River west to the Mississippi. At 1:30 a.m. on the 17th the captain of the stern-wheel steamer attempted to dock at a wharf in Louisville, but heavy rain had swelled the river, and the vessel got caught in a current and bypassed the docking facilities. In a nighttime scenario, the steamer, with more than 200 people aboard, headed for the falls.

The first few feet of *Queen City* nosed out over the falls before miraculously, she struck a rock on the river's bottom and held fast. Unsure how long the vessel would hold her position, the captain blew the whistle for help.

Drazel, who had spotted the disaster, ran down from the lookout, a half dozen flights of steps, and joined Captain Gillooly and the other surfmen in launching *Reckless* and *Ready*. Although they had to pull through freezing temperatures and ice floes an inch thick, both skiffs reached *Queen City* within five minutes. Once aboard, Captain Gillooly calmed the excited and confused passengers, attempting to restore order. He realized that the boat could slide over the falls at any second, and ordered his men to worry about people first, and possessions later. Due to the late hour, some heavy sleepers had to be pulled from their beds in various states of undress, and then led in stunned bewilderment to safety. Gillooly also ordered his surfmen to lower and man the steamer's yawl for use in transporting passengers and crew to safety.

During the night, the intense cold and thick mist caused ice to form in the boats and oars. Besides adding weight to the oars themselves, ice on the oar locks made the oars nearly impossible to move, and ice on the handles yielded no firm grip whatsoever. The surfmen spent most of the night breaking the ice off of their equipment in between runs. By 5 a.m., they had rescued all 215 people aboard.

When a tug pulled the steamer free from its precarious perch above the Falls, the rock she had struck pulled out of the riverbed with her, still engorged in the two-foot hole it had created.

During the deadly floods of March and April, 1913, Surfmen Drazel joined Keeper Gillooly and three other surfmen in responding to distress calls from a number of Ohio River communities. At 3 a.m. on March 27, Captain Gillooly received telegraphic orders from the Treasury Department to take a crew and a boat and head for Dayton, Ohio, where floodwaters reached murderous levels. Before they receded, they would claim 454 dead (150 in Dayton alone), leave 100,000 people homeless, and cause $250,000,000 in property damage between Ohio, Indiana, West Virginia, Kentucky, Illinois, Missouri and Tennessee.

Crossing the river to Cincinnati in the middle of the night, the lifesavers boarded a train, boat and all, and headed to Dayton. They arrived sixteen hours later, and sought out the local relief work director. He informed them it would be pointless to set out to work that night. And the crew should get a good night's sleep and head out at first light. They slept that night in the National Cash Register plant.

At 5 a.m. on the 28th, the crew rowed with 500 rations, delivering food and water where needed, and carrying the sick and crippled to relief. They then toured the northern half of the city, rowing between rooftops, bringing aid to another 800 people in one way or another.

On the morning of the 29th, the floodwaters had receded to a point where the people of Dayton could safely leave their homes. By 2:30 p.m., the town's officials thanked the crew and sent them on their way, on a train back to

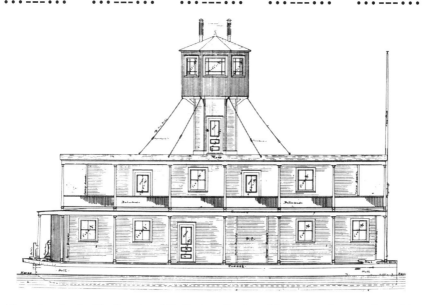

Plans for Louisville floating Life-Saving Station. Three vessels served as this station. These plans are representative of the second vessel. The last one, built in 1929, is still afloat at Louisville. She has been renamed the Mayor Andrew Broaddus. *Nautical Research Centre and the United States Coast Guard*

Cincinnati. They reached their destination by 6 p.m., but had to wait until morning to cross to Louisville.

The next morning, while waiting to cross, Captain Gillooly and his men received a telegram ordering them to nearby Covington, Kentucky, where at least 50 families were in distress. After distributing food to the citizens of Covington, they received yet another distress call. Six miles up the river the town of Dayton, Kentucky, had become surrounded by water, and many houses built on sandy soil had already broken off their foundations and overturned. On the 31st, the Louisville surfmen rescued 75 people in Dayton, before heading back to Covington. By 6 a.m., they received orders to head back home, where conditions had gotten considerably worse. They reached Louisville the next morning, where the surfmen who were left behind to man the station had been working continuously for days. On the third of April at 8:45 a.m., the crew headed out en masse, in a 65 mile-per-hour gale and heavy rain, and attended to the folks of their hometown. At the end of the night, the crew could finally stand down. They had helped well more than a 1000 people over the course of the longest week of their lives.

In his 1921 *Louisville Courier-Journal* profile, William Drazel told of several river events that never otherwise reached newspaper headlines. He once watched in horror as a large steamer backed its rear paddle wheel over a small skiff anchored just off of the river's bank. The two men aboard the skiff got sucked into the water, one of whom managed to free himself and resurface within a few seconds. The other, who could not swim, passed underneath the length of the boat. When Surfman Drazel found him, he pulled the terrified victim, who had been underwater for more than two minutes, to safety. During the entire ordeal, the man had held a briar pipe, which he had been smoking at the time of the accident, firmly clenched between his teeth. Miraculously, both men survived with nothing more than a rapid heartbeat after their unexpected swim.

On June 27, 1916, Drazel witnessed the saddest event of his 40-year life-saving career. Responding to the cries of two young boys whose boat was headed for the falls, Surfmen Drazel and John Munz had their boat smashed to pieces on the dam. His knowledge of the river's waters and his ability to swim saved his life that day, although his clothes were torn to shreds by the sharp rocks of the rapids. Surfman Munz, though, did not survive.

Perhaps due to the death of the young surfman, William Drazel prepared to retire later that year. But, due to the impending intervention of the United States in the war raging in Europe, the Coast Guard temporarily froze all retirements. Five years later, Drazel found that he still had the urge to perform his life-saving duties, and that he still possessed the skills to do so. "I have no hankering for retirement just now. I've been here so long that I wouldn't know what to do elsewhere, and besides I can still pull an oar with the young fellows."

When not saving lives, Drazel liked to fish and read. In 1913, he caught a 67-pound catfish, no surprise to his fellow surfmen, who knew he had a knack for knowing where the "big ones" would be. His friends also said he lived by the motto "a good book is a good friend."

Finally, on April 10, 1922, at 60 years old and with a 40-year career in life-saving behind him, Surfman Drazel decided to retire, receiving his discharge papers on that date. Although Drazel wore only one medal on his chest, Captain Richard Herline of the Louisville station said that he "received the greatest amount of official praise of any enlisted men in the service."

Much more important to Drazel, though, was the respect he earned from his Life-Saving Service and Coast Guard brethren. He gained legendary status amongst the crews of the 10th district, who marveled at his unblemished career. To his fellow lifesavers, he was known as the man who "served forty years without a break in duty."

THE LIFESAVERS
Ida Lewis: Wrecks and Rescues
by Donna Hill (Volume 3, Number 4)

DAVID Atkins, that heroic, tragic USLSS keeper of Cape Cod, had a peer in Ida Lewis, devoted lighthouse keeper of Newport Harbor, Rhode Island, and heroine of many rescues who nevertheless also died believing she was a failure.

Ida Lewis was just sixteen years old when she made the first of her daring rescues. On a rainy, windy afternoon in September, 1858, she looked out from what was then her father's lighthouse and saw four teenagers in a catboat (a type of sailboat) joy riding in the harbor just off Fort Adams.

About half a mile from shore, the sailboat began tossing wildly. One of the boys had climbed the mast and was rocking the boat, in fun or to tease his friends.

Then it wasn't fun any longer. The boat capsized and threw the boys into the water. The boys tried to cling to the overturned catboat, but it would not support them all. They took turns holding on. Watching, Ida knew that the boys would soon be so numbed by cold that they would lose their grip on the boat, go under and drown.

It was growing dark and the sea was rough, but Ida dashed out, shoved off in her skiff, and rowed out to the rescue.

Ida did not look like a robust heroine. She was fair-haired, blue-eyed, slender and scarcely average in height, but had great skill in handling boats, gained from rowing her two younger brothers and sister to school on the mainland in every kind of weather.

Her brother Rudolph once said that Ida could handle a boat in a gale better than any man he ever saw, even when the sea was breaking over her.

43

But now Ida was rowing out to save four teenage boys who were floundering in the sea and no doubt crazy with fear. When she reached them, the boys tried all at once to crawl into her skiff over the side. That would have capsized the boat and thrown her into the water with them.

Ida fended them off with her oar and ordered them to get around aft. One by one she hauled the frozen and exhausted teenagers aboard over the stern and rowed them to the lighthouse. There Ida's mother put them in dry clothes and revived them with a dose of hot

Ida Lewis as she appeared around 1869.
James Claflin

molasses. Later it was Ida, no doubt, who rowed them back to the mainland.

Although the boys thanked Ida and her mother, no thanks came from any of the parents at that time. Perhaps ashamed of their behavior and embarrassed at having been saved by a young girl, the boys never confessed. Years later when Ida was famous, one of the mothers thanked Ida's mother, saying she had only recently heard the story from a witness.

Ida Lewis was born February 25, 1842, and named Ida Wally Zoradia after her mother, the daughter of Aaron C. Willey, a physician of Block Island. Ida's father, Hosea Lewis, was from Hingham, Massachusetts, but moved to Newport in 1835 with his four-year-old son by a previous marriage. He and Ida Wally were married March 17, 1838. They had six children, but the two older ones died in childhood.

For twelve years, Captain Hosea Lewis was a coastal pilot in the U.S. Revenue Cutter Service. Then he was made keeper of the lighthouse in Newport Harbor, which began operating in 1855. The light was on the larger of two little islands known as Lime Rock and Little Lime Rock, a quarter of a mile from shore.

East of Lime Rock lay the city of Newport. On a bluff to the west stood Fort Adams, which came to play an unusual role in Ida's life. To the south were several luxurious estates of summer residents and to the north was the basin where yachts belonging to the wealthy were anchored in season.

At first Lime Rock held only a shed and the lighthouse tower, dubbed the "sentry box," because of its shape. For three years while the family lived in Newport, Ida's father rowed out daily in every kind of weather to tend the light.

Finally, a house was built on Lime Rock and the family moved into it in June 1858. It was a square, white-washed cottage of two stories, with the light at one corner, no higher than the roof. The light, usually called a beacon, was in a projecting window of the structure, with glass on three sides and an excellent view of the harbor, Fort Adams, the mouth of Narragansett Bay and Goat Island. Access to the beacon was through a bedroom closet on the second floor. Compared to other lights then in use, the beacon was small, but it was essential in the ever-treacherous Newport Harbor.

A short time after the family moved to the island, Ida's father had a stroke that so disabled him for the rest of his life that he could not even cut his meat. As was then common when a keeper died or became disabled, his duties fell to his wife or to a spinster daughter. Ida's formal education had to end so that she could help her mother care for her father, tend the beacon, keep the lighthouse in strict repair and handle family responsibilities.

Ida did not let this prevent her from going to the rescue of anyone who needed her. In the winter of 1859-60, Ida saved two soldiers from Fort Adams when their skiff turned over in the harbor. Always minimizing her heroism, Ida said there was "quite a breeze" at the time, but others called it "a living gale."

During the Civil War, Fort Adams and Lime Rock beacon were crucial in coastal defense. Ida and her mother went on courageously tending the light, even when many other lighthouses were damaged or destroyed.

Ida continued her habit of saving people.

In February 1866, three soldiers were returning to Fort Adams after a day on the town when they came upon Ida's brother's skiff moored at the wharf and decided to row across the harbor instead of walking the three miles around on land.

Out in deep water, one soldier put his foot through the boat, which swamped and began to sink. The other two soldiers swam to shore but failed to turn up at Fort Adams. Their bodies were never found. It was assumed they had gone AWOL.

The soldier with the wrecked skiff was pulled rapidly out to sea. Ida saw him, rowed out to the rescue, and found the soldier half-drowned, drunk, and nearly helpless. She injured herself pulling the burly man aboard her skiff, but she got him to the lighthouse, where she and her mother revived him, fed and warmed him and lent him dry clothes. The soldier offered very little thanks and never returned the clothes.

Soldiers from Fort Adams seemed to have a particular penchant for being saved from drowning by little Ida, but they were not the only ones. On a stormy day in January 1867, three Irish shepherds were going through town with a herd of sheep when one of the animals ran blindly out on the wharf, plunged off into the tide and was carried out toward the bay.

Frantic to save it, the shepherds jumped into Ida's brother's new skiff, but they could not handle a boat in a storm and were soon swamped. The boat was drifting out to sea when Ida, who happened to be sewing at the lighthouse window, saw it. As usual, she launched her own skiff into the storm.

She said later the Irishmen were astonished. One of them cried, "Oh, be Jabers, have you come to save us?"

Save them she did, then went back for the sheep, got a rope around the terrified animal and towed it to shore.

Coast Guard painting of Ida Lewis performing a rescue. United States Coast Guard

Not long afterwards, on a bitter February morning, Ida's mother saw a sailboat stranded on a reef with a man in the rigging and the tide up to his neck. Again it was Ida to the rescue. The man told her that his boat had been wrecked the night before and he had been hanging on desperately ever since. Although drenched and frozen, he would not be taken to the lighthouse. Shivering and God-blessing her, he begged to be set down on the wharf, where he went scurrying away on his hands and knees.

Later, Ida learned that the man had stolen the boat. The owner said that he would have given Ida fifty dollars to let the thief drown.

Ida once told a reporter that she was never afraid rescuing people, she just did it and that was all there was to it. By the time Ida was twenty-seven, she had saved ten people, with notice of only a line or two in local newspapers. Then on March 29, 1869, her rescue of two soldiers caught the attention of big city reporters. Her life was changed.

Sergeant James Adams and Private McLaughlin, on leave in Newport for the day, were due at Fort Adams about five o'clock. They were not happy about the long walk around on shore to their garrison. When a fourteen year-old boy offered to take them directly across the harbor in his catboat, assuring them that he could handle it, even in that storm, the soldiers climbed aboard and the boy pushed off.

The boy was not the sailor he claimed to be. About half way to the fort a gust of wind sent the boat rocking. The boy slammed his tiller to the wrong side. The boat capsized and powerful waves rolled it over. The soldiers and their young boatmen were thrown into the sea.

Gasping and freezing, they clung to the catboat's hull. Icy snow lashed their faces. The cold weakened their muscles and numbed their hands. As their boat pulled out toward Goat Island, they saw the cheery beam of the lighthouse recede through the falling snow.

The soldiers and the boy clung to the boat for about half an hour. Then the boy's strength gave out and he lost his hold. Shrieking, he clutched Private McLaughlin, but a wave washed over them and dragged the boy away. Flailing and choking, he went down and disappeared while the soldiers looked on helplessly. The boy's body was never found.

Meanwhile, the Lewis family was at home in their warm, comfortable lighthouse. Ida had a cold and was sitting before the kitchen stove, warming her toes in stocking feet. Her father was in his favorite chair. Her brother Hosea, now age twenty, was nearby and so, no doubt was their seventeen year-old sister, Hattie. Their brother Rudolph, now a sailor age twenty-two, was most likely away at sea.

J. Earl Clauson, writing in *Putnam's Magazine* in 1910, says that Ida heard the soldiers screaming for help and that her mother tried to keep her from going to the rescue. He does not mention Ida's brother, Hosea. George D. Brewerton's biography of Ida, published in the year of the event, says Ida's mother heard the cries, her father urged her not to go, and her brother Hosea went with her. Ida provided a testimonial to the book's accuracy. It seems to be the basis for many articles written later.

According to most accounts, Ida's mother went upstairs to check the light, to make sure the wick was burning properly and to add oil, if needed. By now an experienced lighthouse keeper who had seen many storms, she looked out casually. Then she saw the overturned boat. She rushed downstairs crying to Ida that men were drowning.

Ida jumped up, shouted for Hosea to come along, and dashed into the storm without hat, coat, or even shoes, just a towel around her sore throat.

Ida's mother flew out to the rock to wave to the men and shout that help was coming. Ida's father tried to call Ida back. As a former coast pilot, he knew the peril of a little skiff in a northeaster. Although he had often seen Ida row the younger children home from school in such fierce weather that, as he had said per Brewerton, he would not have bet a penny on their safety, yet he never got over being afraid of her. Now Ida ignored his plea, and so did Hosea.

With her usual powerful strokes, Ida rowed out into the harbor. It had grown quite dark. Wind shrieked around Ida and her brother and sheets of icy water broke over them, but Ida pulled steadily on to the overturned catboat. The soldiers grabbed the side of Ida's skiff and Hosea reached out to help them. Ida ordered them to stop. She said later that she had to whack the men's hands with her oar to make them let go and get around to the stern, where she and Hosea could pull them aboard.

All of Ida's strength and skill were needed to row the loaded skiff back through rough sea to the lighthouse. Sergeant Adams was so weak that he could hardly climb out and get to shelter. Private McLaughlin was unconscious. Ida and Hosea struggled to haul him out of the boat and up to the lighthouse between them.

The soldiers gave Ida a gold watch, in thanks. Their commanding officer, Bvt. Major General Henry J. Hunt, wrote her a letter of appreciation and sent a purse of $218 from officers and men of the garrison. Ida received a

Lifesaver Ida Lewis' home at Lime Rock Lighthouse in Rhode Island. United States Coast Guard

commendation from the State of Rhode Island as well as gold and silver medals from several humane societies.

Harper's Weekly of July 31, 1869, used Ida's picture on the cover, showing her in heroic but uncharacteristic posture, arms folded. The *New York Tribune*, Frank Leslie's and other journals and newspapers spread Ida's fame from coast to coast. Nearly all reports praised Ida's courage and modesty, but the editor of *Harper's New Monthly Magazine* in his "Editor's Easy Chair" was slyly contemptuous. He wrote that no man would be such a "donkey" as to ask if it were unwomanly to "tug and strain through a tempest and then pull half drowned men into a skiff." However, he advised Ida to "get safely married, change her name, and leave the lighthouse before Mrs. Grundy reached Newport."

However, Ida did not lack admirers. As many as a hundred a day came from every part of the country to stand on shore and gape at the lighthouse. Some of them would shout for Ida to row over and get them. Ida's father said that by the end of that summer when he stopped counting, more than nine thousand people had come for a glimpse of his daughter.

Ida was showered with gifts. A present from Maine, oatmeal and maple syrup for her father, was the one Ida liked best, saying she felt that it came from the heart.

Letters poured in, requests for her autograph, her portrait, a lock of her hair, her life story. Poems were written about her, sometimes with many stanzas. People asked to board at the lighthouse. A youth from New York wanted to stay with her, but admitted that he was underage and hadn't yet told his parents.

Men she had never seen proposed marriage. A cadet from West Point named his home-town mayor as reference and sent his father with his photograph to plead for him. The father said that Ida might learn to love his son, but Ida said the boy was a young thing, too adolescent.

Newly-elected President U.S. Grant, passing through Newport, paused at the harbor and sent for Ida to come and meet him and his wife in their carriage. Asked what they said to her, Ida replied that flattering speeches all sounded alike.

The attention Ida got was not all harmless. Pranksters screamed for help in the middle of the night. Visitors to the lighthouse stole her photographs, scrapbooks and other belongings. One even took the painter off her boat.

Ida admitted that she was "slightly ruffled" when the attention interfered with her chores, tending the light, washing, cooking, cleaning and helping to care for her father.

Fourth of July was declared Ida Lewis Day at Newport. People came from all over Rhode Island and nearby states to a celebration held in a park near the harbor. Children turned out in Ida Lewis sailor hats and scarves knotted to the side as Ida wore hers, ready for action.

Francis Brindley, lawyer and classical scholar, presented Ida with an ornate four-oared surfboat named *The Rescue*, a gift from the people of Newport.

The boat was brought to the scene on a dray pulled by handsome horses, Ida was made to stand in it while Brindley proclaimed that she was superior to Caesar, who had only rescued a papyrus from the sea, while she, "with fragile arms, had saved half a score of men despairing in the jaws of the insatiate sea."

Ida asked the abolitionist and feminist, Thomas Wentworth Higginson, to express her thanks, since she had never made a speech and didn't expect to begin now. Higginson said that Ida had saved men from worse than drowning by her work for a temperance union.

After the presentation of a rudder with an inscribed silver plate, two flags, and three cheers, Ida had her new boat lowered into the harbor. She stepped aboard and rowed back to the lighthouse with bold, easy strokes, maneuvering through yachts, small pleasure craft, and working boats. At home, she continued to use her plain, old, practical skiff.

About a year later, on October 23, 1870, Ida married one of her many suitors, William Heard Wilson from Black Rock, Connecticut. He was a sailor, fisherman and captain of a yacht moored in Newport Harbor during yachting season. Ida moved with him to the mainland, or, as some say to

Connecticut, but their marriage was not happy. Ida soon returned to the lighthouse and resumed her duties along with her maiden name, although she and her husband were never divorced.

Over the years, Ida continued to rescue people, eighteen by official count, the last when she was sixty-four. The actual number, however, was thought to be thirty or more. Ida herself didn't count the people she saved, didn't even know some of their names.

Ida's father remained paralyzed until his death in 1872. In 1879, after her more than twenty years of service to the lighthouse, Congress officially made Ida keeper. Her salary was raised from $500 a year to $750, which made her the highest paid keeper in New England. Still it seemed that the Lighthouse Board considered women less than official, since uniforms were issued to the men in 1883, but not the women.

Ida Lewis was honored with a gold life-saving medal by the U.S. Life-Saving Service for her heroic rescues. The 1881 Life-Saving Service Annual Report honored her as winning "national celebrity by her rescues" and notes that her most recent rescue "was accomplished at the imminent risk of the rescuer's life." United States Coast Guard

On February 4, 1881, it was nearly twilight in freezing weather when Ida made another spectacular rescue. Two musicians from the Fort Adams military band tried to cross the frozen harbor on foot. They fell through.

Hearing their screams for help, Ida snatched a rope and crawled out to the men over the breaking ice. The soldiers, Germans with a poor grasp of English, did not understand Ida's instructions. They both grabbed the rope she threw to them and nearly pulled her into the hole. Somehow, after dunking them both, she hauled one of them to safety. Her brother Hosea rushed out to help her with the other.

Members of USLSSHA may be particularly interested to know that the U.S. Life-Saving Service awarded Ida their gold medal for heroism. Their Annual Report of 1880-81 said, "The action on her part showed unquestionable nerve, presence of mind, and dashing courage." The report added that only a short time afterwards, two men fell though the ice in the same area and were drowned.

In spite of so many accolades, Ida was sad in her personal life. Her brave young brother Hosea and her sister Hattie both died of tuberculosis in 1883. Her mother grew sick and weak and died of cancer in 1887.

Ida went on faithfully tending the light. She never took a holiday or even left the island except to do errands, to get mail and supplies, or to attend the Methodist Episcopal Church. She lived alone with her cocker spaniel, Dewey, and six cats, until her brother Rudolph came to be her assistant.

In 1906, Congress voted Ida its Congressional gold medal of honor, first class. The American Cross of Honor Society gave her its gold medal. The Carnegie Hero Fund gave Ida a monthly pension of $30, which at that time amounted to nearly half her salary. The Humane Society of Massachusetts awarded her its silver medal, the first ever given to a woman outside of that state.

Apparently not much impressed by her medals, Ida kept them in her work basket.

When she was nearly sixty-eight, Ida was described as sprightly although complaining that she did not have the strength of her youth.

After some fifty years of heroic service, Ida received a letter dated February 10, 1909, from the Light House Establishment, saying she had made an error in arithmetic in her report of expenditures for oil, wicks and chimneys. The letter ordered her to correct and return the report at once, saying "Exercise more care… errors made by you delay this office in making its report to the Light-House Board."

Although the complaint was trivial, the wording was harsh and Ida took it as a reprimand for failing in her duties. She was devastated.

That and a false rumor that Lime Rock Light was to be abandoned caused Ida such distress that her brother believed they brought on the paralytic stroke she suffered in October, 1911. Ida lay ill while letters and telegrams poured in. The War Department sent orders to the Commandant of the Narragansett Bay Defense District to suspend target practice, so as not to disturb her. The Fall River liner *Priscilla* went by with bells tolling in Ida's honor.

Ida's death three days later was mourned by all of Newport and beyond. Her funeral was held at her church, the Methodist Episcopal. The Seventh

Artillery band played in the street until the service began. Artillerymen were her pallbearers. A steady procession of people viewed her body where it lay in state.

She was buried in the "Common Ground" on Farewell Street, near others of her family.

Although in the end, Ida felt that her life's work was not appreciated, she might have been gratified to know that the lighthouse was renamed in her honor in 1925, although it remained in service only two more years. In 1928, the house and tower were sold to the Narragansett Bay Regatta Association, and became the home of the Ida Lewis Yacht Club.

Bibliography

Bible. *Holy Bible of Ida Lewis*. Collection of the Newport Historical Society. Has family names and dates on the flyleaf.

Brewerton, George D. *Ida Lewis, the Heroine of Lime Rock*. Newport, R.I.: A.J. Ward, 1869. Claims to be attested to by Ida herself; is the basis for many articles later.

Clauson, J. Earl. "A Half-Forgotten Heroine…" in *Putnam's Magazine*, Feb., 1910, pp. 515-523. Differs from Brewerton in details.

Clifford, Mary Louise and J. Candace Clifford. "Ida Lewis at Lime Rock Light, Rhode Island, 1879-1903" in *Women Who Kept the Lights*. Williamsburg, VA: Cypress Communications, 1993, pp. 91-98.

Department of Commerce and Labor. Light-House Establishment. Tomkinsville, N.Y. Letter to Ida W. Lewis, February 10, 1909, from (name illegible), Captain, U.S.N. Inspector. Collection of the Newport Historical Society.

"Editor's Easy Chair" in *Harper's New Monthly Magazine*, June 1869, as quoted in Thompson (see below) p. 94.

"Ida Lewis Struck Down" and ff. *Newport Herald*, Oct. 24, 25, 28, 1911. Collection of the Newport Historical Society.

"Ida Lewis Is Sinking Slowly" *Newport News*. October 24, 1911. Collection of the Newport Historical Society.

Jeffreys, C.P.B. *Newport: A Short History*. Newport, R.I.: Newport Historical Society, 1992.

Randolph, Norris. "Newport's Forgotten Heroine" in *Yankee*, August, 1959, pp. 128-131.

Spears, John R. "Heroines of the Surf" in *Harper's Baazar* (sic), Aug. 18. 1900, pp. 991-994.

Thompson, Sue Ellen. "The Light Is My Child" in *Log of Mystic Seaport*, Vol. 32, No. 3, Fall, 1980, pp. 90-98.

United States Life-Saving Service. Annual Report of the Operations, Fiscal 1880-81, p. 87.

Walford, Herbert Ladd. "Ida Lewis" in *The American Magazine*, 69 (1910) pp. 334-337.

THE LIFESAVERS

"One of Nature's Noblemen": Keeper Walter Nelson Chase of Nantucket

by Mary Miles with Maurice Gibbs (Volume 2, Number 2)

NANTUCKET history has a way of wrapping its tendrils around you and never letting go, never letting you say "the end." A story that began as a short biographical sketch of an interesting Nantucketer, Walter Nelson Chase, has now grown to a longer piece including a bit of the history of the island's Life-Saving Stations, the "humane houses" (houses of refuge), and Nantucket's most famous rescue. When I moved into the second-floor apartment of a 200-year-old in-town house, people would ask me if I was living with any ghosts. I'd answer, "None that have made themselves known to me... yet!" But certainly there have been interesting people who have lived there.

The two former residents of the house most often mentioned to me are the late "Aunt Charlotte," a well-loved Nantucketer I wish I'd known, and "the Skipper," or Keeper Walter N. Chase, whose life and adventures form the kernel of this story. He lived here with relatives of Charlotte's family from some time after his wife died in 1912 until his death in 1928. Keeper Chase was a bona fide Nantucket hero.

Walter N. Chase was born in 1852 to William H. and Mary J. Chase. The name Chase is well tied into island history; there are 24 listed in the most recent phone book, many of them descendants of the first Nantucket families. Walter was grandson of the famous Owen Chase, survivor of the whaleship *Essex* which became the grist for Herman Melville's tale, *Moby Dick*.[1] Walter's life was firmly tied to the sea, and in his 30s he became one of the first and finest surfmen at the new Coskata Life-Saving Station, commissioned in 1883. This was one of five stations operated by the U.S.

Life-Saving Service within Nantucket County. By 1886, Chase would become its second keeper. In 1887 he married Lydia B. Morris (1844-1912). She, too, would become an integral part of life and service at Coskata Life-Saving Station.

Nantucket Island's surrounding waters are famous for their dramatic history of shipwrecks. Between 1877 and 1915 alone, there were more than 200 shipwrecks. The treacherous and picturesquely named shoals (Old South, Old Man, Rose and Crown, Handkerchief, Davis, New South, Long,

Keeper Walter N. Chase.

Tuckernuck, Muskeget) and rips (Old Man's, Great Point, Miacomet, Bass and more) and shallows (Black Flats, Coatue Flats, Tuckernuck, Fathom Bank, to name a few) became the graveyards for many souls, ships and cargoes. By the last quarter of the 1800s a public-spirited islander, Frederick C. Sanford, was bringing strong pressure to bear to build lifesaving stations. As the leading member of that early life-saving organization, the Humane Society of the Commonwealth of Massachusetts on Nantucket, he was seeing to it that the humane huts (houses of refuge) and stations were improved to help cope with the repeated disasters and misfortunes of this period.

Early Massachusetts Humane Society "huts of refuge" and stations, abandoned and forlorn during the traumatic Civil War years, were in need of refurbishment or outright replacement. As a result, between 1874 and 1886 a number of these were built or rebuilt through the efforts of Sanford and other civic leaders. Massachusetts Humane Society humane houses were put up or refurbished at Siasconet, Smith's Point (then known as Great Neck), Kroskaty Farn (Coskata), Tuckernuck Island, Quidnet, Forked Pond, the Head of the Hummock, Tom Nevers Head, and the Nantucket Bar. Stocked with food, blankets and basic supplies, these rough and sturdy structures often had heavy lines (ropes) strung out by stakes to the water's edge. The idea – which worked on occasion – was that if not-quite-drowned sailors made it to land after a wreck on some dark, stormy night, they might find and follow the line to shelter. The chance of surviving a shipwreck and then perishing before help could come was very likely, even if one did reach land. Though some Massachusetts Humane Society structures (Tuckernuck, Siasconet, Sankaty and the Nantucket bar, to name a few) did have boats and some even beachcarts, they were not necessarily manned. Many seamen didn't survive when washed ashore. There are awful stories of townspeople finding lifeless victims in the island's sands following storms.

Between 1874 and 1891, Nantucket had four USLSS stations in operation at one time or another, plus a fifth temporary "station." The number is five if the temporary station on Tuckernuck Island, located not in a real station building but in a former residence, is counted. The original Muskeget Island station, built in 1883, was destroyed by fire in 1889. For two years an interim station was manned on Tuckernuck Island, site of an early Massachusetts Humane Society station. The Tuckernuck Island "hut of refuge" still stands, now owned by an island family as their "hide-a-way". In 1874, largely through the efforts of Frederick C. Sanford, the Massachusetts Humane Society's committee head on Nantucket, Sumner I. Kimball would authorize the first station, Surfside, at Point-o'-Breakers area at Surfside on Nantucket's exposed south coast. Next built were two stations in 1883, Muskeget and Coskata. Muskeget Island would cover the treacherous namesake channel between that island and Martha's Vineyard. At the northeast corner of Nantucket Island, Coskata would do double duty, monitoring the eastern Nantucket Sound as well as the shoals east and east-southeast of the island.

On December 28, 1889, a vicious storm was sweeping over the low sand of Muskeget when fire broke out. To the crew's credit, most equipment was saved, but little could be done as the building went quickly in the gale. Plans for a station at great neck (now Madaket) for 1891 now had to include rebuilding Muskeget, one of the most isolated island spits of sand along the New England coast. Both stations would be Bibb #2 designs. In the interim a fifth unplanned station was established on Tuckernuck Island by leasing existing buildings. The temporary Tuckernuck station, never an USLSS-designed building, would operate for more than two years until a new permanent station was built at Muskeget.

When Coskata Station was commissioned in 1883, its first keeper, Civil War veteran Benjamin Pease, was a logical choice. He chose young Walter Chase as his No. 1 man. In that first winter, Chase justified his keeper's choice during a number of daring rescues. On February 20, 1884, Keeper Pease, Chase, and the other surfmen had a unique chance to prove their mettle. The brig *Merriwa*, with Captain J.S. Adams, was headed for Boston from South Amboy, New Jersey, loaded with 420 tons of coal. After trying to ride out a nor'west gale near Handkerchief Shoal, it struck at Great Point Rip and found itself in a black and dreaded place seamen called Rescue Holl at about midnight. The Coskata crew set out, braving the cold seas, and managed to rescue all on board. From launch to return, the crew had traveled over 6 gale-ridden miles in their fragile craft. The rescue under such conditions was further complicated by a most ungrateful bunch as had ever washed ashore. Once back at the station, the *Merriwa* crew showed little thanks. Becoming roaring drunk with liquor they'd brought off the wreck, they stole everything not tied down including some of the lifesavers' pea coats. By the time they had been delivered to town the following day many altercations had occurred. Years later when Chase was 75, he recounted to the then-Commodore of the Nantucket Yacht Club that this motley band was still quite drunk on the following day: "Before they left the station, we took three revolvers away from them – but not until a couple of them fired them." When the Commodore asked, "What did the lifesavers do when that happened?" Chase replied, "Well, we didn't want to see anyone shot – so we had to use a bit of persuasion."

While transferring the *Merriwa* crew to town, "persuasion" took a more severe form. Chase and the owner of the catboat delivering them were forced to hold one crewman at bay with a shotgun. Not all sailors were properly grateful to their rescuers.

In 1886, Chase succeeded Benjamin Pease as keeper of the Coskata Life-Saving Station. Considered fair but tough, he was used to commanding, being listened to and receiving respect. It has been written that Walter Chase had a 6'4" frame with a 6'4" voice to match. Several of the old crew remained at Coskata when Chase took over. One new man was known as a slacker and troublemaker. Chase's standards were high and he tried to get the surfman removed, but political circumstances prevented this. He remarked philosophically, "A government job is like pudding – you have to take the sauce along with it." However, Chase drilled his crew so rigorously that it wasn't long before the problem surfman "couldn't stand the gaff" and was very happy to be transferred elsewhere.[2]

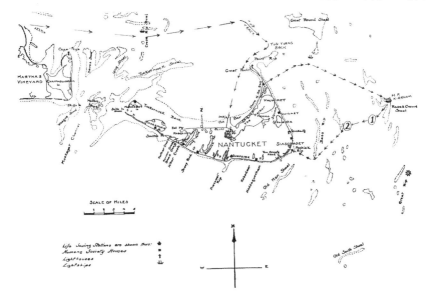

Map of Nantucket and other islands, showing track of Coskata crew, plus that of the tug that turned back in heavy seas. The number "one" denotes the first anchorage and the number "two" the second anchorage of the surfmen.
Nantucket Life-Saving Museum

The Coskata crew was alert, well-trained, loyal, and courageous to a fault. On the night of January 20, 1892, they were ready for anything, maintaining regular patrols in spite of the snow squalls and sleet. Early in the morning of the 21st, the station phone rang. It was Keeper Joseph Remsen of Sankaty Head Lighthouse five miles south of Coskata. A few hours before, he had seen what he thought were flares on Bass Rip; now, in the morning light, he could see the rigging of a ship, a ship that was plainly in trouble. As it turned out, the vessel was foundering further out on Rose & Crown Shoal, ten miles east of Bass Rip. And it was not flares Remsen had seen, but mattresses dragged into the rigging of the *H.P. Kirkham*, a British schooner, whose desperate crew had set them alight in a last-ditch effort to attract help.

After a hurried breakfast, Skipper Chase and his surfmen – Jesse H. Eldredge, John Lyman, Charles B. Cathcart, Josiah B. Gould, George H. Flood and Roland H. Perkins – pulled the surfboat on its carriage across the beach and launched it on the ocean side of Great Point. Chase had phoned town to request the assistance of a tug, which, it turned out, never arrived owing to the heavy seas. He knew his surfboat would have to return from the shipwreck into headwind and seas. It would be tricky and extremely dangerous, but neither he nor his men hesitated. His wife, Lydia, took up the watch at the station and said her prayers. One of the verses of a hymn sung by the Unitarian Church choir at the ceremony honoring Skipper Chase and his crew a year later seems relevant here: "And while they wrought so long, a woman kept her watch/At station or at lighthouse near, with hear of prayer/And self-forgetting love the latch/Oft lifted on the door of secret Altar-stair."

By the time Chase and his men arrived at the scene of the disaster, at around 11 that morning, the *Kirkham's* hull was under and seven men were in the rigging. The water surged and the tide pulled; there was real danger of the surfboat becoming entangled in the schooner's rigging. But perhaps most perilous of all was the problem of safely getting the frightened and thoroughly soaked *Kirkham* crew aboard the surfboat. The frozen sailors, at the end of their strength, were so anxious to get into the surfboat that when they received the line delivered with the heaving stick, they immediately began hauling on it so hard that the lifesavers' surfboat almost swamped. Skipper Chase thundered: "Stop hauling – stop, I say! Make your end fast. If

Part of the gold medal crew, as they became known locally, following presentations. Left to right, Josiah Gould, "Skipper" Walter N. Chase, Jesse Eldridge, George Flood, and Charles Cathcart. John Nyman was "off island" when the ceremony occurred. Roland Perkins was deceased, dying as a result of exposure during the rescue. Nantucket Life-Saving Museum

you make one more pull on that line we'll cut it!" And he handed his knife to his bow oarsman.

He said later, "The poor fellows had been in the tops'l all night, and had been 15 hours on the wreck…. We figured on their dropping into the boat when the waves lifted us up. It was close figuring, as their rail would be down six feet under water one minute and then that much above us on the next wave. They had to time their jump for the right moment – if they had jumped when we were under – by Jove, that would have done it."

The return was the worst part of all. The wind was again piping up. Keeper Chase ordered the mast and sail thrown overboard – with fourteen souls in a raging sea, the surfboat rode low in the water and freeboard was critical. The surfmen had to struggle to clear the shoal, all the time moving about the sick and helplessly numb survivors lying in the bottom of the boat. Twice on the return it was necessary to anchor, to wait for the south tide to move them toward shore. Had they not, the north tide, coupled with the northwest wind, would have dragged them seaward. It did not improve anyone's spirits to watch the *Kirkham* break up and disappear only a few miles astern.[3] Constant bailing was necessary, and almost everyone was sick, ice forming on hair, eyelashes and clothing. The anxiously awaited tugboat did not come! Ten hours had now passed since the Coskata crew left their station. With the temperature hovering near 12 degrees, darkness was setting in and the snow squalls were increasing in strength. Yet from time to time they could see the Sankaty Light flashing. The keeper allowed his men to sleep for short periods, one by one, but all knew that the chances were great that they would not make it. Nantucket was still 11 miles away and to wind'ard! It was a terrible night. Finally as it grew light, conditions improved slightly. The sun broke through the clouds and Chase urged his men to pull steadily at the oars – hour upon agonizing hour, accompanied by the groans of the sick and scared schooner crew. It was his compelling confidence and encouragement that kept the hopes of the surfmen up, and their trust in his seamanship and judgment. Finally, 26 hours after launching the surfboat at Coskata, they reached the coast at the village of Siasconset, seven miles south of their departure point. All the villagers were on the beach to assist – they had waited long anxious hours, and now shouted with joy and relief as they watched the red surfboat draw near and land.[4] "Tell my wife we have safely come ashore," said Chase, and then, after he made sure that his boat was pulled up out of the water, he helped carry the victims to warm and welcoming little 'Sconset cottages.[5]

Lydia Chase had been heroic also, maintaining the watch back at the Coskata Life-Saving Station – all alone, with her hopes waning by the hour. When the call came that the men were safe, she could hardly believe it. Onlookers said that when she finally was reunited with her husband she grasped him and tenderly pulled his face down to hers, looking into the eyes she had imagined she would never see again.

The men – rescuers and rescued – had all survived that January night, but there was a victim after all. Surfman Roland Perkins developed pneumonia following the ordeal. His fellow crew members and Keeper Chase watched anxiously as he weakened. Weeks passed, and the men were notified that they would receive medals of honor from the government. "When are the 'stovecovers' coming, Skipper?" joked Perkins from his bed, probably knowing he wasn't going to pull through. He never saw his medal. It was a year before the award ceremony took place and by then the brave "Perkie" had been dead for nine months.

On January 8, 1893, the Unitarian Church on Orange Street, just up from Main, was crowded to overflowing. Each surfman received a large, heavy silver medal with its deep blue ribbon. A gold medal with its vermilion ribbon was presented to Captain Walter Nelson Chase. The official commendation from Charles Foster, Secretary of the Treasury and the General Superintendent, Sumner I. Kimball, detailed the rescue in every particular, ending: "You displayed superb seamanship, unerring judgment and dauntless courage… skill and unfaltering fidelity to duty, and… heroic disregard of danger." Schoolgirl Emma Nickerson recited "A Race for Life" by J.L. Molloy, which included the lines:

A gun is heard at the dead of night,
"Lifeboat ready!"
And every man to the signal true
Takes his place in the eager crew,
"Now lads, steady!"
First a glance at the shuddering foam,
Then a look at the loving home,
Then together, with bated breath,
They launch their boats in the gulf of death…

It was more difficult to learn about the civilian life of the retired Walter Nelson Chase than about those momentous 26 icy hours off on the Rose and Crown in which he and his crew proved they were true Nantucket watermen. In the years after he retired as keeper of Coskata Life-Saving Station, he

Coskata Life-Saving Station, spring or summer of 1893. Keeper Chase is in the formal blue uniform at right while his surfmen wear the "summer white" informal uniform. Nantucket Life-Saving Museum

continued to be an active, useful member of the island, including serving as a selectman from 1911 to 1913. On January 21st, 1915, a friend and fellow lifesaver, Reuben Small, met him in the street and asked, "Do you know where you were 23 years ago today?" Said Chase in a letter to a friend, "As he (Small) stood smiling and awaiting the result of my mental calculation, it occurred to me that between 12 and 1 o'clock upon January 21st, 1892, I was anchored alongside the *H.P. Kirkham* in that life and death struggle in which we came out victorious. Dear! Dear! How the time goes."

You can stop along the Polpis Road to Coskata today at the Nantucket Life Saving Museum and see the medals of Walter Nelson Chase and his three gallant surfmen, George H. Flood, Jesse H. Eldredge, and the only victim of that momentous rescue, Roland H. Perkins. You can also make a final stop in your peregrination into Nantucket history at the Prospect Hill Cemetery where so many surfmen's government markers indicate their final safe harbor. There you will also find Walter Nelson Chase's final resting place beside his beloved Lydia. True to his uniqueness as a lifesaver among lifesavers, his grave is marked differently with a rough bronze plaque saying:

Walter Nelson Chase

1852-1928

As Keeper of Coskata L.S.S. he led his men in the memorable rescue of the crew of *H.P Kirkham*, wrecked on Rose and Crown Shoals Jan. 20, 1892. Recipient of Gold Medal from the government for outstanding bravery. He was one of "Nature's Noblemen."

THE LIFESAVERS
The Life-Saving Guns of David Lyle
by J. Paul Barnett (Volume 2, Number 1)

THE idea of throwing a weighted line to an otherwise inaccessible place must be contemporary with the invention of rope itself. Surely the idea has occurred spontaneously to every schoolchild. The use of mechanical ordnance to cast lines prior to the invention of gunpowder would be more surprising in absence than in presence.

Attachment of a line to a powder-expelled projectile to establish communication with a stranded vessel seems to have been seriously advocated by Sergeant (later Lieutenant) John Bell, of the British Royal Artillery. Bell's concept was that with line contact established, the initial whipline could be used to pull a hawser and attendant rescue tackle out to the ship, for transportation of the crew over the surf to safety.

Sergeant Bell demonstrated his idea in 1791. Using a mortar with a line attached to the shot, Bell cast the line 400 yards, and proposed that British ships be fitted with similar mortars. Bell was commended for his idea, but it was regarded impractical: the mortar weighed 600 pounds, and the shot 60 pounds.

After experimentation with lines cast from lighter pieces of ordnance, Captain George W. Manby, also English, established that Bell's idea had been valid. In 1809 Captain Manby rescued the crew of the brig *Nancy* with a line attached to a smaller projectile fired from a mortar much lighter than Bell's. Though Manby later died in poverty, with even a mortgage on his own tombstone, between 1809 and the time of his death he saw life-saving stations built along British coasts as the result of his work.

With the idea of shotline rescue accepted, the search for better ways of effecting it began. In 1829, John Dennett, of the Isle of Wight, proposed that lines could be better carried by rockets. Using a modification of the 18th century Congreve rockets ("the rockets' red glare"), Dennett devised two line-carrying rockets: a single 9-pounder and a twin 12-pounder. The 9-pounder lacked range. The 12-pounder had range, but became the cause of concern if only one tube fired, in which case it tried to come right home.

There were advantages of portability and other factors in favor of rockets. But they were badly affected by moisture, tended to be erratic in flight, contained a

Lieutenant David Lyle. United States Coast Guard

built-in fire hazard, and reportedly sometimes burst instead of flying. Rockets had a design advantage in that a crosswind surging across a line would tend to steer a rocket into a compensating course. But the shotline, given the greater density of the line-carrying shot, could be stably aimed to compensate for crosswind.

In the 19th century a contest developed between rockets and mortars for dominance in the field of line rescue. Colonel R.A. Boxer, also English, developed a two-stage rocket that combined the best features of both of Dennett's rockets. The French experimented with various devices, and settled on two types of mortars. In London, kites were manufactured for getting lines from ship to shore, on the theory that any wind that would drive a ship aground would also carry a kite to shore. Some rescues seem to have been accomplished with kites. Manby system mortars remained in use.

With the establishment of the U.S. Life-Saving Service in 1876 under Sumner I. Kimball, an effort was begun to develop an effective and standardizable system of projecting lifelines to distressed ships. The person appointed to conduct that effort was Lt. David A. Lyle.

Lyle was an 1869 West Point Academy graduate. By 1877, he had been on arsenal duty at the Benicia Arsenal near San Francisco, on frontier duty in Alaska, and on cavalry escort duty in Death Valley. When called upon to develop a line-carrying appliance, he was back at West Point, as a professor of experimental philosophy. Lyle's assignment was to conduct the new project "in addition to his regular duties." Starting with "an old rifled howitzer found among a lot of captured ordnance," Lyle first experimented with projectiles suggested by the Ordnance Board, slotted along one side to allow slipping the line down the bore alongside the projectile.

Lyle's first firing ground was in Springfield, Massachusetts, at what is now Van Horn Park. Firing from what is now the vicinity of 314 Chapin Terrace, and complying with an agreement to post guards appropriately on the road to Chicopee, which bisected the range, Lyle was able to establish a test field for shooting. A few shots with the rifled howitzer and the slotted projectile established that was not the way to go.

Captain Manby's mortar projectile had been a 5-1/2 shot of round or other configuration with a plaited hide leader attached. The leader was to prevent scorching of lines by the blast of expulsion. Drawing on Manby's idea, Lyle began experimenting with projectiles built with an iron shank instead of the hide leader.

One of the arguments that favored rockets over mortars was that mortars, being fired at high elevation, consumed great quantities of line in order to reach fairly short distances. Rockets could be fired in a flatter trajectory. Since laying out the line was tedious, line consumption was important.

Lyle saw small howitzers, fired at rocket-angle elevation, as the most promising route of experimentation. The heavy projectiles for Lyle's experimental guns took on a sash-weight-with-eyebolt configuration. Inserted into the muzzle with the shank protruding from the muzzle, the projectile turns 180 degrees on departure, taking the line trailing behind it.

First at Springfield and later at Sandy Hook, New Jersey, Lyle conducted tests in 1877 and 1878. Using bronze castings of his own design, poured under his supervision at the South Boston Iron Works – a company descended from the Cyrus Alger Foundry of Civil War fame – Lyle made three guns of similar configuration but of different sizes. He named them Bronze Gun A, Bronze Gun B and Bronze Gun C. The bores were of 3-inch, 2-inch and 2-1/2 inch diameter respectively. The carriages were of simple iron-bound wood design. Since they were to be set in sand, they had no wheels. Bronze Gun C became the Lyle Gun.

They Had To Go Out...

The designs were audacious. An ordinary 2-pounder (2-1/2 inch bore) with carriage could be expected to weigh a hundred times or more the weight of its loose-fitting round shot. Lyle's "sashweight" projectile weighed 18 pounds. The whole gun weighed 163 pounds, nine times the weight of the shot. Additionally, the shot was machined to a piston-like fit in the bore, instead of being a traditionally loose smoothbore fit. The combination of an extremely lightened gun, an uncommonly heavy projectile, and the air-tight fit of the projectile, all combined to create sharply rising breech pressures, and uncommonly heavy recoil.

All gunpowder then in use was black powder, a simple chemical mixture dating back to the Middle Ages in Europe, and earlier elsewhere. (Modern "smokeless" powders are sophisticated chemical compounds yielding infinitely greater pressures.) Of the grades of black powder available, Lyle chose one of the milder: Hazard's Navy Cannon Powder. With that coarse powder, recoil was kept within reason, and pressures remained safe. The service range of the gun came to be about 1200 feet. Later regulations set the test performance range at 1050 feet.

Concurrent with Lyle's experiments, Robert P. Parrott, by then one of the grand old men of American ordnance, had developed and patented a 3-inch lifesaving mortar. Edmund S. Hunt, of Massachusetts, had developed a gun whose projectile carried a self-contained line that payed out in flight. Some Hunt guns and at least 25 Parrott mortars were placed into shore service, but were later superseded by Lyle guns. Some of Hunt's gun/projectile combinations came into use on ships. Lyle tested the Parrott and Hunt systems.

In the fall of 1878, Lyle made his recommendations, and Lyle guns at once went into production for distribution to lifesaving stations. References to their use make dramatic appearance in the winter of 1879-80, when a storm reaching from Louisiana to Maine created a general shipping disaster.

By 1890, the American Carrier Rocket Company, of New Bedford, Massachusetts, had undertaken production of Cunningham line-carrying rockets employing self-contained lines much like the Hunt system. Lyle guns also came to supersede those.

In 1889, Congress passed an act requiring line-carrying devices to be placed aboard steamships. The shipmasters didn't want them. A controversy arose. The Board of Supervising Inspectors of the Steamboat Inspection Service was caught in the midst of multi-sided arguments among rocket makers, gun makers, steamship owners, Sumner I. Kimball, Congress, and the Secretary of the Treasury. The Board cited the opinion of no less than "the

68

The 1878 model Lyle gun - Bronze Gun C - with line carrying projectile. This was the type of Lyle gun used by the U.S. Life-Saving Service and early Coast Guard.
J. Paul Barnett

Honorable Sumner I. Kimball, whose judgment in such matters will not be questioned in any part of the civilized world," to the effect that Lyle guns could not "be used, or carried on shipboard, without subjecting the passengers and crew to dangers not less appalling than shipwreck itself." But it set specifications for Steamboat Inspection Service approvable Lyle guns.

Under pressure from the steamboat lobby Congress repealed the 1889 requirement in 1891, after which time the Lyle gun placement aboard steamships became customary, and then required around World War I. Sailing ships were not affected either way, and some irregular line throwing appliances, in addition to approved ones, may have been made for that market.

The first major modification of Lyle guns for steamship use came at the hands of William F. Coston, son of Benjamin Franklin Coston and Martha J. Coston, of Coston Signal Company fame (as of 1900, the Coston Supply Company). According to William R. Baack, 92 years old as of 1970 and 52 years a Coston employee, production of Coston system Lyle guns began with their patented invention around 1895, and ended shortly after World War I, with over 2000 units produced.

Surrounding facts seem to support that recollection. Martha Coston, in her 1886 autobiography, *A Signal Success*, gives copious detail about the company and her son William, but makes no mention of Lyle guns. An early Lyle gun bears the letters "PAT'D" cast into the left sideplate. Coston Lyle guns with serial numbers approaching 2500 have been seen. An 1895 patent would have expired around World War I, allowing competition from other makers.

Coston system Lyle guns have triangular metal sideplates joined together with tiebolts, and a barrel of standard 2-1/2 inch Lyle bore anchored between the sideplates at the peak of the triangle. Elevation is accomplished by means of a link attached between the cascabel of the barrel and an arc of holes drilled in the sideplates to allow variation by removal and replacement of a sliding pin.

The second prominent modification of Lyle gun design came through the efforts of a young eastern inventor, Francis Granger Hall, Jr. An 1899 Yale graduate with a degree in electrical engineering, Hall's career of invention lasted into the 1930s, and included the underwater arc light used in salvage of the *USS Maine*, various marine engine appliances, improvements in shoulder-fired lifeline guns, faking tubs in which lifelines were coiled for shipboard Lyle gun use, various types of breech-loading Lyle gun, and improved emergency vehicle lighting, which possibly refers to the rotary safety light.

At Wolf Trap Farm National Park for the Performing Arts near Washington, D.C., a group of 16 Lyle guns stand ready for use in an authentic performance of Tchaikovsky's "1812 Overture." Guns are fired in accordance with the 1880 musical score by electric switchbox as intended in the original 1880 plan. J. Paul Barnett

Taking on part of the problem of Lyle gun recoil around 1902, Hall placed trunnions at the breech rather than at the midpoint of his barrels, in order to change the center of gravity and direction of recoil thrust. It helped. In configuration, Hall system guns are sometimes mistaken for military mortars. Placement of trunnions at the breech with sliding-pin elevation forward of that point allowed Hall system guns to close flat like a jackknife, to facilitate stowage. Aboard ship, any Lyle gun had to be lashed in order to limit recoil.

After Hall's patent expired around 1919, other companies hastened to compete with Hall's Naval Company using Hall system guns of comparable design. Those companies came to include the Steward Davit and Equipment Corporation (Model B); Reading Iron and Steel; the Driggs Ordnance Company; the Sculler Safety Corporation; Kent Marine Products; McKeever-Daley; Heat Transfer Products; and the Hawley Smith Machinery Company.

Coston system guns made after expiration of the Coston patent include ones by Steward (Model A); C.C. Galbraith & Son; David Kahnweiler's Sons; the Hilyard Company; and F.G. Hall's own Naval Company.

There may be others of both systems as yet undiscovered. The Landley Company for instance, is given as an approved maker, yet nothing has yet appeared on what type of Lyle guns that company may have made. In two known instances, approved makers say they never made a Lyle gun; one of those says it never manufactured anything at all.

Aside from Coston and Hall system guns, there were commercial spin-offs from Bronze Gun C. The American Ordnance Company which manufactured 105 Lyle guns on government contract in 1900, produced later commercial ones with identical Bronze Gun C barrels but with steel carriages modified for shipboard use. Others were produced in varying grades of approximation by D. Kahnweiler, the New York Gun Company, E. George & Company, and possibly other makers for use aboard ship.

Producers of Bronze Gun C projectiles were of case iron, machined cylindrically with an ogival nose and a frustum at the point of shank attachment; shanks were of machined wrought iron. Commercial projectiles were generally made of ordinary cold-rolled steel round stock, flat on both ends, with shanks variously made of 5/8 or 3/4-inch steel rod.

Between 1878 and World War II, a host of factors converged to make the charging of Lyle guns a delicate matter that ended calamitously in a number of instances. Hazard's Cannon Powder became DuPont Lifesaving Powder. Sometime before World War I, the Steamboat Inspection Service changed its approval wording to "black powder," which let in the fast burning sporting grades: Fg, FFg, FFFg and so on. A 1952 or so Coast Guard manual refers to "Black, Grade A-1, Cannon" powder, which was at best vague. A fundamental gain in potency from improved purity of chemicals (sulphur, salt-peter, and charcoal) seems to have occurred at the turn of the century. Measuring a fine grained powder in a cup cut for a course grained powder results in a greater weight of charges thrown, in addition to faster burning.

In 1878, Lyle had warned against any forcible jamming of projectiles on seating, saying that crushed granules of Hazard's Navy Cannon Powder could create "all the violence of a fine powder: such as ones he had rejected as too potent in his 1877-78 tests. In 1946, cursory tests by the U.S. Coast Guard delivered up to 47 feet of recoil from an 1878 model Lyle gun. Lyle had regarded recoil of over 14 feet as "severe."

In 1971 and '72, civilian trials of the three main types of Lyle guns indicated that 2-1/4 ounces of DuPont Fg black powder did the work of Lyle's 1878 charges of about five ounces of Hazard's Navy Cannon Powder.

In related conversations, Roger C. Hale, retired chief of the Merchant Marine Technical Division of the U.S. Coast Guard during World War II, concurred that the 1971-72 tests seemed germane to accidents that his office had been obliged to examine – other than ones that had involved substitution of various modern "smokeless" powders for black.

In 1994, charges of about 1-1/2 ounces of Goex Fg black powder, common today, yielded projectile ranges, with the line attached, of about 750 feet with moderate recoil.

By late in World War II, controversy again enveloped the Lyle guns. England by then had developed a workable line-carrying rocket that was proposed as superior to Lyle guns. Lyle guns were used in scaling cliffs during invasions, but so were rockets. The old problems of rockets were still there in the new ones, but technology had diminished them. Use of Lyle guns involved antiquated procedures and cumbersome equipment, and was time consuming.

In 1947, the Coast Guard – which over the years had come to have authority over all line-carrying appliances – yielded to the arguments for rockets. In 1952, the 1947 approval certificates for the few remaining makers of Lyle guns expired without renewal.

Except for the very last years, David Lyle's own life spanned the life of his 1878 accomplishment. From 1882 to 1902, he was an inspector of ordnance, during which he made contributions in metallurgy, guns, carriages and projectiles. In 1884, he received a degree in mining engineering from the

The Manby Mortar. Barely legible inlaid plaque reports mortar's use in first recorded rescue with line throwing ordnance in the United States, saving 201 lives from the wreck of the Ayrshire *at Squan Beach, New Jersey, on January 12, 1850. J. Paul Barnett*

Massachusetts Institute of Technology. From 1902 until his retirement for age in 1909, he commanded the arsenal at Augusta, Georgia, where he was also chief ordnance officer of the Atlantic and Gulf coasts. His retirement rank was colonel.

David Lyle was a member of many professional clubs and societies, and was awarded the rank of chevalier in the French Legion of Honor for his work at the Paris Exposition in 1889. His books included his Report on Life-Saving Apparatus (1878), Manufacture of Leather (1878), and with Samuel W. Porter, Manufacture and Uses of Files and Rasps (1881). He published more than eighty papers on professional, ornithological, and geological subjects, and was special editor of *Funk and Wagnall's New Standard Dictionary* of 1913. Lyle was also a philosophy professor at West Point.

His most lasting single contribution remained the Lyle guns. A 1908 report on his career, written by Sumner I. Kimball, still General Superintendent of the U.S. Life-Saving Service, credits Lyle guns with being fundamental in the saving of nearly 4500 lives of shipwrecked persons in the USLSS alone. By the time of Lyle's retirement, Lyle guns were in worldwide use.

David Lyle died at St. Davids, Pennsylvania, in 1937. He was 92.

THE LIFESAVERS

"Those Guys Got Plenty of Guts, Take It From Me": Hilman J. Persson and the Rescue of the Crew of the Trinidad

by John J. Galluzzo (Volume 5, Number 1)

AS a young boy growing up in Sweden at the beginning of the twentieth century, Hilman John Persson could never have dreamed of what the future held in store for him.

Born September 3, 1888, Persson first stepped foot on American soil at eighteen years old in 1906, sponsored for citizenship by his uncle Mattis Persson, a surfman at the Gray's Harbor Life-Saving Station in Westport, Washington. His only assets at that time consisted of a sturdy frame and a definite desire to find work. His greatest liability was his complete inability to speak English.

After a short, uncomfortable, and unhappy stint pushing logs through an Aberdeen sawmill, Persson followed his uncle's advice and began work as a temporary surfman at the Gray's Harbor Life-Saving Station, keeping himself available as a substitute to fill in when others became sick or had to attend to family concerns. Recognizing the young man's competence in the required skills of the U.S. lifesaver, the station's keeper, Captain Charles Jacobson, hired him to a full-time position before the end of 1907.

Two years later Persson married Eliza Jane Armstrong, a member of one of Westport's pioneer families. Together they raised two healthy boys, Nathaniel and Fridolph, although, sadly their only daughter Minnie died at just seven years old.

Soon the years spent in the Life-Saving Service added up to form a decade. In 1915, as the Life-Saving Service merged with the United States Revenue

Cutter Service to form the Coast Guard, Persson realized that he had found his life's career path. In 1919, at thirty, he accepted a transfer to the Willapa Bay, Washington, Coast Guard Station as second in command, "where he got some experience being in charge because Captain Winbeck, as he was known, was on sick leave a great deal of the time." (Memoirs of Fridolph Persson, in the possession of the Westport Maritime Museum, Westport, Washington, p. 1). In 1922, upon the death of the skipper of the Gray's Harbor station, Persson transferred back home again, to take his first command. There he would remain until 1938.

Persson's reminiscences of his early working life echo those memories of most Life-Saving Service and Coast Guard surfmen. Working for low pay with little chance for advancement under the motto "You have to go out, but you don't have to come back," many of the lifesavers of the chronically-underfunded services nevertheless remained loyal to their jobs, either for fear of joblessness or simply because of the personal satisfaction gained by knowing theirs was a humanitarian trade.

"At the time I joined the lifesaving service, none of the boats at the station were equipped with motors because no dependable small gasoline motor had been invented yet, and besides, we were always slow in receiving up-to-date equipment. We, the oarsmen of the station, considered ourselves fortunate because, in going to the assistance of a vessel in distress, there was nearly always a seagoing tug at the Westport dock that we could depend on towing us to the scene. The vessel could mean a case of salvage for the tug and we could assist in getting a tow line to the vessel if she was stranded in water too shallow for the tug.

"Unfortunately there were many times when there was no tug available, as they always left for their headquarters in Hoquiam on Saturday afternoon for the weekend unless there was a vessel expected. This was the case one Saturday night when two Westport brothers were hunting ducks near the old County dock in South Bay. They were sitting close together in a sinkbox when one of the guns fired and most of the pellets hit the other man in the abdomen. This was before there was a road to Aberdeen, and we were called upon to get him to a hospital. The only means was the lifeboat under oars and we pulled hard all night, arriving at the Hoquiam dock at daybreak, where it was discovered the man was dead. On questioning, the brother said he had died about halfway to town, but he was too shook up to say anything." (Memoirs of Hilman John Persson, in the possession of the Westport Maritime Museum, pp. 1-2).

Bos'n Hilman Persson, center, finally gained recognition for his years in service in 1937, after orchestrating the rescue of the crew of the Trinidad. *Coast Guard Museum/Northwest*

By the late 1930s, after three decades with the Life-Saving Service and Coast Guard, Persson thought he had seen it all. He had been in for so long that he began to lose track of how many missions he had been on, how many lives he saved, and where exactly most of the ships sunk in the area rested. In 1910, he aided in the rescue of the crew of the British bark *Torrisdale*, saving thirty men. Twenty years later, he reported, "we were trying to get a stranded fish boat off the beach at that spot and nearly hit the encrusted hulk with our boat in the trough of the sea. I thought she was buried long ago." (Memoirs of Hilman John Persson, p. 1).

Some things he had learned the hard way. "For sometime we had been transporting the Willapa Harbor Pilot to and from steamers entering or leaving the harbor. Our boat had a sliding canvas hood in the bow, which afforded some shelter from wind and sea, but the steerman was in the open.

"One cold winter day, around 1921, we were returning from putting the pilot aboard an incoming vessel about three miles west of the harbor. The ship was out of sight as she traveled much faster than we could, when a blind break, a sea breaking without warning, came over the stern. This knocked me away from the rudder and we became waterborne. The boat, as was usual without rudder, broached and I went over the side. When I finally located the boat it was about a quarter of a mile away."

"We had failed to put on life preservers, as they were of cork sewn to a canvas belt that slipped over the head and tied with straps and were very cumbersome in a boat, especially over winter clothes. I was dressed for the cold and over my normal underclothing had on a pea jacket, rubber hipboots and oilskin trousers and coat. All of these clothes became soaked, I was floating pretty low in the water. I was treading water and determined not to panic or to swim towards the boat as this would have been impossible burdened as I was."

"The Captain had gone to the rudder and one of the crew heaved a preserver overboard as they came towards me, but a breaker swept it away. I managed to get a hold of one on the second try and in about ten or fifteen minutes I was picked up. After that experience, there was no more transporting pilots by the station boats." (Memoirs of Hilman John Persson, p. 7).

Still, after thirty-plus years of stormy seas and battered ships, risk taking and lifesaving, Persson's defining moment had yet to come.

On Friday, May 7, 1937, "Captain" Persson set his crew about their daily tasks. At 8 a.m., they sent up the morning colors. Between 8:15 and 9:00, they ran through their typical resuscitation and fire drills. As the temperature rose to sixty by noon time, one man mowed the station's lawn, while the rest of the on-duty personnel tackled fence, truck door, and boat repairs. At sunset, as he ordered the colors down for the evening, Persson noted a slight change in the wind's direction, from southeast to south. By 8 p.m., the light winds from early in the day had steadily grown to a force eight gale, more than sixty miles per hour.

At 8:10, after inspecting the grounds, Persson fielded a telephone call from the Willapa Bay (North Cove) station to the south. From the watchtower at Willapa Bay a surfman had spotted an unidentified steamer shooting off flares, obviously in distress. He reported, too, that the station's powerboat had already left on another emergency call, rendering assistance to a fishing vessel. At 8:30, after dispatching a message to the district commander of his intentions, Persson rounded up a crew of four – Motor Mechanics Roy I. Anderson and Jesse W. Mathews and surfmen Roy N. Woods and Daniel

Hamalainen – and set out on motor lifeboat *3829* to find the imperiled mariners. For Hamalainen, this trip represented his first actual search and rescue case.

An hour and a half after launching, they crossed the bar out of Gray's Harbor and turned to the south, taking notice of the strong northerly current. Instructing his four crewmen to watch for any signals from either the steamer or Willapa Bay lifeboat, Persson crawled into the cramped quarters of the forward compartment to monitor the radio, a receiver only. "This is the most uncomfortable place on a boat, with the bow diving and pounding into the sea and I did not want to subject any of the others to this torture." (Memoirs of Hilman John Persson, p. 8). Before leaving the station, he ordered that the boat be called every fifteen minutes. No useful news was reported.

Miles to the south, the steam schooner *Trinidad*, destined for San Francisco with a full load of lumber, battled the storm. "Head on into a sixty-mile gale went the vessel, staggering like a drunken man... her flexible hull had yawning seams, and her master would have bet on a stack of holystones that his crew had pumped the entire North Pacific through her hull twice." (James A. Gibbs, *Pacific Graveyard*, p. 152). After several hours of battering by the sea, she rode hard aground atop a submerged shoal one mile to the west of Willapa Bay Lighthouse.

When she struck, the lumber on deck broke loose, smashing and slamming its way through the ship's sides. The

Hilman Persson's uncle Mattis sponsored him for American citizenship, and then coaxed the young man to join the Life-Saving Service. Westport Maritime Museum, Westport, Washington

second mate, Werner Kraft, lost his footing and flew overboard, perishing in the churning seas. The remaining crew of twenty sailors gathered on the bridge, hopeful that their captain, I. Hellestone, would find a way to keep them all alive.

Around 3 a.m., Persson glimpsed a flare in the distance, and answered with one of his own. Bringing the *3829* around, the lifeboat crew headed for the *Trinidad*. All told, "for fourteen miles, lifeboat *3829* battled walls of water, shaking herself like a wet poodle and going back for more" (Gibbs, p. 153).

At daybreak, around 5 a.m., they reached the North Spit of Willapa Bay finally able to see the damned vessel. While the lifeboat was crossing the South Spit to come around to calmer water, a high breaker engulfed *3829*, submerging her completely pushing her back. Looking for a safer route, Persson "noted an oil slick coming from the stern of the vessel from her ruptured fuel tank, and as oil is supposed to calm breaking water, I followed this in the next try." (Memoirs of Hilman John Persson, p. 9). Coming around the bow to the starboard side, the Coast Guardsmen finally found calmer water.

Calmer water, but not necessarily calm. Careful to steer clear of the ship's rigging, which by now hung over the side in the water, Persson and his crew began their rescue procedure. "Each breaker brought with it the power to crush the lifeboat against the side of the wreck, but by moving in at the opportune time and pulling out with each swell, the lifeboat somehow managed to remove twenty-one crew members from the bridge." (Gibbs, p. 153).

One of the sailors saved from the *Trinidad* gave this description to the *Aberdeen World*: "It didn't look like we would get away alive, then just about daylight the Coast Guard began working in… and were we glad to see 'em. I don't believe I ever lived a happier moment in my life than that, when they came up under the lee side. Captain Persson was hanging on with one hand and waving directions with the other. The boat would rise up on a sea and then plunge down in the trough… I was afraid sometimes they would never come up again but the boat would bounce up like a cork, and kept inching in closer. To this hour I don't see how they made it. They would claw their way up to the *Trinidad*, take off a couple of men and then the sea and wind would beat them away. They would haul around and pitch and roll their way back again and take off two or three more men. We almost prayed for them. They could sure take it and come back for more. And it wasn't only the sea… there was rigging and gear plunging around, masts swaying, loading booms, lumber, and any minute that fore deckload was due to go… but they didn't pay much attention to it... which was plenty lucky for us. Those guys got plenty of guts, take it from me. I'll praise them to my last day."

Making contact with the oil screw vessel *Ruth E.*, Persson arranged for it to transport the *Trinidad* survivors back to their port of debarkation, Raymond. At 6:40 a.m., *3829* arrived at Lakeland, and the crew headed for Willapa Bay Station. At 8 a.m. Motor Machinist's Mate Albert Canaris, just reporting back to Westport from leave, immediately headed for Willapa Bay by truck to retrieve the exhausted crew. At 9 a.m., twelve and a half hours after heading out, Persson, Anderson, Mathews, Woods, and Hamalainen finally returned home.

On September 20, 1937, the crew of *3829* stood proudly on the deck of the USCG Cutter *Onondaga*, before family, friends, and fellow Coast Guardsmen. After a short address to the gathered crowd of more than 100 people, Captain R. W. Dempwolf, Commanding Seattle Division, presented each man with a Gold Lifesaving Medal, the United States' highest award for the rescue of life from danger at sea, and a congratulatory letter from Secretary of the Treasury Henry Morgenthau.

A few months later, Persson left on a ten-day furlough, and headed for the East Coast. Stopping at Washington, D.C., he attended yet another medal ceremony to accept the Second Division Post, American Legion of Baltimore's Medal of Merit, an annual award for the most outstanding act of heroism in the United States, on behalf of the Gray's Harbor crew.

But before he headed home, and while he still had the time to do so, Persson wanted to make one more East Coast stop. Going directly to the west as he had in 1906, he had lost contact with his sister Adina for 31 years, and by now he had a younger brother, born in the United States, whom he had never met. He felt the time had come to see his family again.

And so in March of 1938, Hilman Persson made his way up Nantasket Avenue in Hull, Massachusetts, turning left on B Street to look for house number thirty-four. He knocked on the door and when it opened, for the first time in more than three decades, he came eye-to-eye with his sister Adina Halvorsen. That day he also met his younger brother Berger Persson.

Before leaving Hull, he visited the Point Allerton Coast Guard Station, the historic home of Keeper Joshua James, on a tour of inspection hosted by the station's commanding officer, Captain Isaac L. Hammond.

Shortly after returning to Washington, Persson transferred to the Coast Guard's district office in Seattle, retiring there in 1939, after thirty-two years of service. Before he transferred, though, he convinced his son Fridolph to join the Coast Guard at Westport, to continue the tradition of having at least one Persson at the station from the time of its commissioning. At the outbreak of war in 1941, he rejoined the Coast Guard, remaining on active duty until the end of hostilities in 1945. On December 28, 1944, Technician 5th Grade Arnold W. Halvorsen, U.S. Army, Adina's son and Hilman's nephew, died in battle in Belgium. A street in his hometown in Hull, Massachusetts, is now named for him.

Hilman John Persson died at eighty-four years old on December 20, 1973, after a steady decline in health. In the words of his son Fridolph, "He came to the United States a young, naive boy, but became a loyal patriotic American to the end of his life."

THE ISSUES

•••--••• •••--••• •••--•••

The Humane Society of the Commonwealth of Massachusetts

by Maurice Gibbs (Volume 3, Number 4)

WE speak proudly of the early U.S. Life-Saving Service, as well we should. Its humanity and quiet heroism is legend. Yet, the USLSS was not created from a vacuum. It had a remarkable forerunner – an organization of persistence and dedication to the same humanitarian ideals. That organization preceded the USLSS by many years. When the USLSS finally came along, it was able to draw from the rich experience of the Humane Society of the Commonwealth of Massachusetts, or as it is more commonly known, the Massachusetts Humane Society. Today, many are unfamiliar with the vital role of this illustrious organization.

In 1785, fully eighty-six years before the founding of the U.S. Life-Saving Service, and three years before the Constitution was to go into effect, a group of New England citizens were pondering the troubling issues of human suffering and needless death. How might victims be saved from the calamities of shipwreck, drowning, and other perils? These were the same citizens who had fought and shed blood at Bunker Hill. Some had been with the "embattled" at Lexington and Concord, firing "the shot heard 'round the world." Some had survived the awful English prison ships for their opposition to King George III. These men were revolutionaries in many ways. Within ten years of the Revolution's frenzied start, they would meet, as they often had, at the Bunch of Grapes tavern on Boston's historic State Street to consider other issues, the problems of the suffering of their fellow man.

History records that a blind English Doctor Moyes met with a group of Boston's stalwarts at the tavern during the early winter of 1785. Dr. Moyes

•••--•••

Tuckernuck (Massachusetts) Humane Society House of Refuge #57 on Tuckernuck Island off Nantucket. During USLSSHA's second annual conference, members visited this structure and had a hearty breakfast courtesy of owners Mr. and Mrs. Hamilton Heard. Maurice Gibbs

had arrived from England in May 1784, and was most conversant with the newly-formed British Royal Humane Society (1774). He provided a copy of their objectives and by-laws to his American friends, Royall Tyler, the Rev. James Freeman, and Dr. Aaron Dexter. (Dr. Dexter had been one of those who survived an English prison ship in Halifax). After a series of meetings at the tavern in December 1785, the organization was duly instituted. A formal meeting was called for January 5, 1786, to elect its first officers. The "Humane Society of the Commonwealth of Massachusetts" was in being.

James Bowdoin, governor of Massachusetts, and founder of Bowdoin College, was elected first president of the Society. The officers and trustees read like a "who's who" of the American Revolution. The officers and trustees included Dr. John Warren, whose brother Dr. Joseph Warren had devised the plan of "one if by land, two if by sea": Rev. Dr. Simeon Howard, Dr. Thomas Welsh, Dr. Isaac Rand, Rev. Dr. John Lathrop, Rev. Samuel Parker, Dr. Benjamin Waterhouse and Dr. Aaron Dexter. Another prominent American signing on as an officer of the Society was Judge Oliver Wendell Holmes. Annual membership subscriptions provided the funds to move the

Society forward in its humanitarian work. Among its early subscribers were notables like Boston's leading silversmith and Grand Master of Masons in Massachusetts, Paul Revere.

But what of lifesaving? The Society's leaders had many ideas and actions to pursue. Resuscitation would be their first focus. They recognized that many near death from drowning or overcome by smoke or gases ought to be revived if proper techniques could be devised. The trustees set about offering financial awards to any who could develop acceptable lifesaving strategies. A number of the concepts put forward would place the victim in greater jeopardy than had they been left alone. Curiously Dr. Jonathan Waterhouse, a medical doctor and trustee, would state in 1790, "To blow one's own breath into the lungs of another is an absurd and pernicious practice." The important thing was that serious investigation had begun. It may have been trial and error at first. It would yield results.

The Massachusetts Humane Society would also set up an awards system to encourage humanitarian acts of lifesaving. The first recorded action was a premium of "twenty-eight shillings to Andrew Sloane, for saving a boy from the peaceful waters" of Mill Dam. Its first gold medal was awarded to Lieut. Scott, of his Most Christian Majesty's ship the *Leopard*, for risking his life,

Rarest of the rare. The last surviving Massachusetts Humane Society beach cart now on display at the Nantucket Life-Saving Museum. Nantucket Life-Saving Museum

in jumping from the stern of said ship, then in the harbour of Boston, and saving the life of a young lad, etc., a gold medal, (costing) two pounds, twelve shillings, eight pence." These were the first of over three thousand seven hundred awards given by the trustees through two centuries.

The Society's next area of focus was the result of tragic shipwrecks in and about the coastal approaches to Boston Harbor. A number of persons had survived the shipwrecks, reached the shore of a desolate beach or isolated island, only to succumb, undiscovered, of exposure. A solution had to be found, and the Society had the answer – "huts of refuge." The first three huts were built in 1787, one on the west end of Lovell's Island in Boston Harbor, the second at Scituate Beach on a particularly isolated beach to the south, and the third on the outer beach of Nantasket, a notoriously dangerous coastal strip on the southern extremities of the harbor. Bedding, foodstuffs, a means of lighting a fire, and directions of how or where to go or signal for help would be contained in these essential but austere structures. From that meager start, seventeen would be built at such critical coastal sites and isolated islands by the early nineteenth century.

The Siasconset, *one of four surviving surfboats of the Massachusetts Humane Society. This boat survived on Nantucket Island at the Humane Society's 'Sconset station #53 from 1870 until purchased by the Ford Museum of Dearborn, Michigan. It was returned to Nantucket in 1995 and is in the Nantucket Life-Saving Museum collection.* Nantucket Life-Saving Museum

The Board of the Humane Society of the Commonwealth of Massachusetts in 1998. Seated, left to right: John E. Lawrence, George P. Gardiner, President Francis H. Burr, W. Nicholas Thorndike and William Saltonstall. Standing, left to right: Richard M. Cutler, Charles F. Adams, Dr. Curtis Prout, Ferdinand Colloredo-Mansfield, Frederick S. Moseley III, Charles Devens and Lawrence T. Perera.

In 1807, the Massachusetts Humane Society would embark on its most notable venture, a shift from passive strategies to active rescue work. Construction of lifeboats and mortar stations was ordered. Volunteer crews were organized and equipped to conduct active rescues. The Society's first lifeboat was ordered from Nantucket whaleboat builder William Raymond. The Society's overseer in Nantucket, Captain Gideon Gardner, supervised construction and shipped the boat to Cohasset where it would serve the approaches to Boston. The boat was a near copy of an English lifeboat constructed at South Shields and resembled what was known as a "Greenland boat." It was liberally fitted with cork inside, as well as along the gunwales. She was rowed by ten men, double banked, and was equipped with steering oars at each end. A number of "huts of refuge" were retrofitted with the boats, beach carts and other equipment. Where needed, new buildings were added. The limiting factors in building more stations was often a lack of funds. Yet, by the eve of the Civil War, the Society reported a total of sixty-one lifeboat and mortar stations.

They Had To Go Out...

Not all of the Massachusetts Humane Society's efforts would be focused seaward. As early as 1796, it was instrumental in establishing the Boston Dispensary to serve the needy of Boston and surrounding communities. In response to the great Yellow Fever epidemic of 1799, it would offer a premium to any person able to devise a way of defeating this scourge. The Society would be instrumental in the establishment of Massachusetts General Hospital and awarded Harvard University a grant to purchase a telescope. Improvements in the knowledge of heavenly bodies would thereby improve navigation.

The interior of hut of refuge #56 at Seasachaca Pond, Nantucket. One of four surviving huts on Nantucket, it was originally #51 (circa 1859) and was then six miles north on Great Point. As huts were moved, lost to storm and fire, renumbering was common. Maurice Gibbs

It was recognized that many lighthouse keepers needed equipment and could be a useful resource as rescuers. After all, they occupied some of the most isolated sites in southern New England. Many keepers would have their meager allowance from the federal government supplemented by the Society. It is interesting to note that by 1869, two years before the establishment of the U.S. Life-Saving Service (1871), the Massachusetts Humane Society would report a total of 92 structures in its inventory. Some were lifeboat and mortar stations, others "huts of refuge" – a remarkable testimony to the dogged persistence of its leadership, and by then the unique guidance and energies of its Chairman of the Standing Committee, Captain R.B. Forbes.

The Massachusetts Humane Society was a model for what would follow across America. In local New England waters, leaders of the Society would become the cadre of professional keepers hired to man the new USLSS stations. Already famous as Society lifesavers, such legendary leaders as Joshua James of Hull, Thomas Sandsbury of Nantucket, and other heroes of this volunteer organization would be among the first USLSS keepers. New England had no lack of seamen to serve as crew. Proven watermen from the Society's ranks and others, tried by fire in the Civil War, would make up a large segment of the new service in New England. Throughout his active life, Captain R.B. Forbes would serve as an advisor to General Superintendent Sumner I. Kimball. Information would flow between the old and new organizations. To be sure, there was a rivalry and competition. Each organization would vie to be first at the scene of a wreck. This competition offered many advantages. Neither organization could cover all situations, especially during major gales, when distressed ships outnumbered potential rescuers. At these times, teamwork would result in more lives being saved than either organization could accomplish on its own. Some of the greatest rescues of the last half of the nineteenth and first decades of the twentieth century were accomplished through the joint efforts of both remarkable organizations.

In the early 1930s, the Massachusetts Humane Society began a final drawdown of its last twelve stations. The Commandant of the U.S. Coast Guard reluctantly acknowledged that the day of retirement from this facet of lifesaving had indeed arrived. It would henceforth be left to the Coast Guard to carry on the proud traditions begun by the Society.

Today four surfboats of this brave period survive. Keeper Joshua James' *Nantasket* is on exhibit at his old station, now the Hull Lifesaving Museum; *Siasconet* is at the Nantucket Life-Saving Museum; *Sankaty*, a second Nantucket boat, is on exhibit at the Mariners Museum; and a fourth boat is at

Mystic Seaport. The only surviving beach cart, also from the Siasconet Massachusetts Humane Society station #52, is in the collection of the Nantucket Life-Saving Museum. The private papers and artifacts of the Massachusetts Humane Society are spread among a number of historic sites. Some are held by the Peabody Essex Museum in Salem, Massachusetts. The Massachusetts Historical Society has significant holdings, as do the Hull and Nantucket Life-Saving Museums. A unique challenge awaits any historian or graduate student willing to research and catalog these fragmented holdings.

The Massachusetts Humane Society maintains its offices in Boston. A telephone recorder promptly reminds all callers that it does not deal with the care of animals. Its great humanitarian work continues, especially in support of the medical field. Awards continue to be made to private citizens of the commonwealth who risk their life and limb to save another.

THE ISSUES
Surfman Versus Keeper: Confrontation at Point Reyes Life-Saving Station
by Dewey Livingston (Volume 1, Number 3)

IN June of 1891 the Superintendent of the 12th U.S. Life-Saving Service District, Thomas J. Blakeney wrote to General Superintendent Sumner Kimball in Washington regarding the curious and disturbing mass resignations at the new Point Reyes Life-Saving Station in California. He enclosed letters from the keeper and the statements of three surfmen with grievances against the keeper. The letters, obtained from the National Archives, provide a fascinating insight into the lives of surfmen at a troubled life-saving station in the late 19th century.

Point Reyes was an isolated location for all who lived there. While only about 40 miles north of San Francisco, travel by sea and land was difficult with rugged surf conditions and terrible roads. Scattered dairy ranches, dotting the rugged coastal hills, provided fresh butter by schooner to the city, and a lighthouse stood at the far western promontory. It was windy, foggy, cold, and most of all, lonely.

The station at Point Reyes had been constructed on a long stretch of wild Pacific beach in 1889 but did not operate until the following year because of delays in obtaining a keeper. District Superintendent Blakeney finally nominated William L. Loch to take the position of keeper and Loch moved with his wife into the empty keeper's quarters in April of 1890; they spent three months cleaning, planting a garden and readying the station for active use.

Loch's inaugural crew of seven arrived in July; three left immediately upon seeing the place. Perhaps it was the location or the weather, or perhaps it was Loch's handwritten addition to the printed Articles of Engagement For

Surfmen, "that there may be withheld from each of us the sum of ten dollars per month... until the end of the term of this enlistment, and that no part of the amount so withheld shall then be paid to us unless the keeper shall be able to certify that we have remained at the station and performed all the duties required of us..." With a total pay of $50 per month, Loch was withholding 20% of the surfmen's paychecks, to be repaid at his own whim.

With a replenished crew by mid-July Loch's troubles were only beginning. By October, all seven surfmen had been replaced as a result of their complaints about treatment at the station. Charles Green charged that Loch had tried to kill one of the surfmen, and complained that "I have never suffered so much abuse from any man...." His fellow surfmen attested to the fact that "we found the treatment of Captain Loch unbearable."

Loch defended his actions, blaming the "sea lawyers" among the crew, stating that "the whole crew's motive was to make trouble in order that they would get their discharge, as they often complained to me that the place was lonesome and they also disliked to patrol the beach." Loch implied that at least one of them was afraid of the surf at Point Reyes and unwilling to admit his cowardice.

The trouble continued. The surfmen were appalled at the treatment of fellow lifesavers who had died in the 1890 incident when the huge wave killed two surfmen as they dragged their boat up on the beach. Graves of these dead surfmen in the dunes behind the station remained disrespectfully unmarked and unfenced. According to the first to resign in 1891, Surfman William Andkjer, Loch considered that "(the dead surfmen's) people would not assist and therefore he thought he would not do so himself."

Later Loch found Andkjer and Jonas Robinson fighting, after which Andkjer deserted to the nearest town and, according to Loch, "carried on in a most disgraceful and drunken manner." Days later Andkjer returned and begged for reinstatement, which was denied. He then wrote to District Superintendent Blakeney how Loch "refused to let me have my clothing, giving as his reason that I was indebted $5 (for a) mess bill, and ordered me off the premises. I was obliged to borrow money to reach the city, and am yet without my clothes or means to get others."

Keeper Loch then reacted to Andkjer's written complaint by forcing his surfmen to sign a paper of faithfulness, at which another surfmen left in disgust. The already rebellious crew became more and more on the edge until three, Surfmen Bailey, Samuels and Robinson, left together. Each had his own story.

The Point Reyes Life-Saving Station as it appeared new. The men are probably Keeper Loch and his first crew of 1890. United States Coast Guard

Surfman Alfred T.R. Bailey

That spring Loch mysteriously advanced Bailey to Surfman No. 1, bypassing others more deserving of the rank. Uncomfortable with this, Bailey protested. He was then asked by the keeper to tattle on his fellow surfmen. "He called me and said, 'Alfred, I want you now that you are No. 1 to let me know all the conversation that transpires during the day so I can think it over in the evenings and see if any trouble was likely to come out of such conversations.' I said, 'Captain Loch, I cannot do anything so unmanly as that to eat, sleep and converse with my mates and then repeat to you their conversation....'"

After that Loch found fault with all Bailey did, then abruptly demoted him back to No. 6 surfman. "(Loch) was consistently finding fault, abusing and making use of bad language and throwing his hands about in a very threatening manner and acting like a maniac making my life a complete torture." Loch threatened prison if anyone left, but Bailey warned that "I shall go to the city and see Major Blakeney. I feel sure that he is in total ignorance of the brutal and harsh way you're treating your men.' Loch gave a fiendish laugh and said, 'Major Blakeney would not listen to you, if he did he would spit it all out again.'"

Surfman Samuel R. Samuels

Loch called Samuels "useless" and didn't like that he was a card-carrying member of the Marine Firemen's Union. Samuels charged that Loch extorted money from the crew, and that Loch shot at him during the night beach patrol. The act which made Samuels leave the station was the threat of violence by Loch: "The man had murder in his eyes."

Samuels wrote later to Blakeney saying "you may feel sure that it was no trivial matter that caused me to leave May 26th, for my term would have expired June 30th.... Captain Loch seemed to have a mania for always creating trouble with his crew." Samuels and the others noted how, after a particularly ugly incident, Loch apologized, saying, "May God strike me dead right here, boys, if I treat you harshly anymore."

Surfman Jonas Robinson

Robinson, the No. 2 surfman, claimed that because he was an "application man" he was disliked by Loch. One day he was suddenly disrated to No. 7 for leaving the boathouse doors open; after this while sweeping "(Loch) dogged me around and was tantalizing me I could do nothing right not even hold a broom." After Loch snatched the broom away, Robinson left saying, "let me get away from this detestable place."

Keeper Loch wouldn't allow Robinson to take his clothes. Samuels rose to Robinson's defense, accusing Loch of "haul(ing) a man round the house like a dog." At this point Loch apologized and asked Robinson to stay on as No. 2, but, according to Robinson, "he has been going around like a cat watching a mouse." Soon after, Robinson, Bailey and Samuels left, walking more than 18 miles to the depot. Robinson ended his testimony saying, "in conclusion I must say it is the most cat & dog place I ever was in."

A week later, Alfred Bailey, in a plea for past wages, told District Superintendent Blakeney that "I am thoroughly respectable and always bore a good character, I liked the service very much and would like to go back but not under such a man as Captain Loch of Point Reyes; he does not know how to treat a man...."

Two weeks after the testimony of Surfmen Robinson, Samuels and Bailey was given, Keeper Loch replied to the charges, "...I unhesitatingly pronounce them a prearranged and various pack of vexing fabrications combined and framed by these men with an evil motive particularly designed to throw reflection on me... they have resorted to this malicious method of making false charges in view that they will be countenanced and these misrepresentations will enable them to get their pay from the department, which is the sole object aimed at."

Of the May 26 rebellion, Loch related how Samuels stormed off, saying "to hell with the work, I am off to San Francisco: and tried to get the others to desert. Bailey joined the rebellion, then Robinson left his post at the tower stating, "by God I am off too as we are all Englishmen and will stand by each other."

Loch obviously thought poorly of his crews. "My experience of every man that has been engaged at this station is that they come only for a make shift and they are entirely without money during the year that this station has been manned. I have had to provide them with groceries and provisions as they had no money and it was impossible for them to get credit. After they are here a month or so it is a daily occurrence to hear them making unnecessary comments about the loneliness of the place, hard beach to patrol, too far from town, no liquors allowed on the station and other obstacles that does not meet their approbation which are too contemptible to mention.... Then they get exceedingly careless and try to slight their duties as an opportunity offers.

"I admit that I exact of every man to perform his duties in a satisfactory manner as I consider that everything appertaining to a lifesaving station must be kept in first class condition, I always show my men a good example...." Loch provides examples of not being repaid for groceries, of his men bragging about slighting their duties, of carelessness with loose powder, of one man leaving a lit pipe in his drawer, of sand in the patrol clock and fear on beach patrol. "I must state that I have had a great deal of annoyance at this station with shiftless men who come here to make a few dollars and then flit." Loch rested his case. It was now in the hands of his friend and superior, Thomas Blakeney.

District Superintendent Blakeney than asked the U.S. Life-Saving Service's top administrator, General Superintendent Sumner Kimball's help in making a decision. Directing praise towards Keeper Loch, Blakeney recommended that the surfmen be considered deserters and be treated accordingly. "I have no question of the substantial truthfulness of the statements made by the keeper, and that the men became uneasy and dissatisfied because of the isolated location of the station." Evidently no action was taken for some time. By spring of 1892 the men had not been paid or replied to, so they each wrote pleading for their back pay and their honor; they surmised that Blakeney had not forwarded their letters to Kimball. Not until September, well over a year after the events, Kimball decided "after full consideration," to give them their pay, although less the 20% noted in Loch's handwritten addendum to the Articles of Engagement.

Was Keeper Loch the monster portrayed in the letters from the surfmen, or were the men conspiring to get out of duty at the station? Evidence presented in the archives may produce a verdict against Loch, alleged to be an unstable and violent man, who was accountable to no one by benefit of the station's isolation. The story may ring true for other life-saving stations in the country. Although there are usually bad apples in any kind of group, Loch's record for keeping a proud crew was dismal. It should be noted that after Loch's departure the chaos ceased, no other surfmen died during the Life-Saving Service years, and under subsequent keepers Point Reyes Life-Saving Station built one of the most admirable and courageous records of rescues in the nation.

THE ISSUES

African-Americans in the U.S. Life-Saving Service at Pea Island, North Carolina

by William D. Peterson (Volume 1, Number 4)

Editor's Note: National news stories in 1996 called attention to the posthumous presentation of gold life-saving medals to the African-American surfmen of Pea Island Life-Saving Station in North Carolina. Coast Guard Commander Stephen Rochon, 15-year old Kate Burkhart of Washington, North Carolina, and two college teachers, David Wright and David Zoby, all contributed to efforts to give just recognition to the heroic surfmen of Pea Island. Two ceremonies were held, one at Pea Island Keeper Richard Etheridge's gravesite on Roanoke Island. Along with Coast Guard Commandant Admiral Robert E. Kramek, the descendants (grandchildren and great-grandchildren) of Pea Island surfmen attended the ceremonies. Recognition was, all agreed, long overdue. Although African-Americans served at several North Carolina life-saving stations, only one station, Pea Island, had an all-black crew. Their famous rescue of the schooner E.S. Newman *on October 11, 1896 was particularly acclaimed, though many other heroic rescues were conducted by the Pea Island crew.*

WHY did the African-American crews of the Pea Island, North Carolina Life-Saving Station receive a posthumous award of merit from the United States Coast Guard only last year? The rescuers recently recognized had performed their duties from 1880 to 1914. Why honor those men of the U.S. Life-Saving Service today? Had their work been overlooked in the past? Was the posthumous award given for courageous service at a time when contributions by African-Americans might have been ignored?

The Pea Island station was located along what is today the Cape Hatteras National Seashore. Through the years, the record of the Pea Island crew was

Pea Island Life-Saving Station's surfmen rolling out their surfboat for a drill. United States Coast Guard

impressive. In 1884, the Pea Island station is mentioned in the wreck of the schooner *Exel*:

"The sailboat *Exel*, employed in carrying the mails between Manteo and Kinnakeet, North Carolina, was caught in Pamlico Sound, on the 5th, by a violent snowstorm, and the occupant of the boat compelled to leave his craft about a mile from the Pea Island station, coast of North Carolina, and to seek refuge at that station. But for the shelter afforded him he must have perished. The storm continued until the night of the 9th, when the wind changed suddenly to a strong gale from the southwest. The boat being deeply laden sank at midnight, and most of the contents were washed overboard. The crew of the station reached the boat early on the morning of the 10th and succeeded in raising it and bringing to the shore. They also recovered about two-thirds of the cargo...."

The efforts of the Pea Island crew were noted. Appreciation of the efforts of the Pea Island crew, from the master of the vessel, crew and female passenger of the *Charles C. Lister, Jr.*, is evident in a letter addressed to General Superintendent of the U.S. Life-Saving Service, Sumner I. Kimball:

"Sir: We came ashore in the morning of the 22nd in heavy north-by-west gale, and we want to inform you of the timely heroic service that was rendered us by the crews of the Oregon Inlet and Pea Island stations. They bravely did their work in saving our lives, landing everyone safe, and we join in sincere thanks to the crews for this and for the kindness and care we have received since we have been here. They were abreast of the schooner within forty-five minutes from the time she struck, for which rapid work they should receive credit that truly belongs to them. If they had not been on hand we should likely have all been lost. We also thank the keepers and crews of the New Inlet and Bodie's Island stations, who arrived in time to render much assistance in rescuing us."

The stories of the Pea Island crew are many. The following information is excerpted from the United Life-Saving Service Annual Reports, regarding the activities at the Pea Island station.

Wrecks of the schooner *Emma C. Cotton*, December 27, 1895 and schooner *Maggie J. Lawrence*, February 10, 1896:

Emma C. Cotton - Stranded at 2 a.m. during shift of wind, 200 yards from shore. Alarm was given and station crew hastened to wreck with beach apparatus. Prepared to fire shot line on board, but master of schooner hailed keeper and requested that action be deferred until daylight. While waiting, keeper sent for surfboat, and at daybreak an attempt was made to launch it, which was successful, and schooner was boarded. Took off the crew of seven men with their baggage and landed them without mishap; carried them to the station, where they were succored for three days. On January 2, saved the sails of the schooner, assisted by crew of Oregon Inlet Station. Vessel and cargo were a total loss.

Maggie J. Lawrence - Stranded during strong northwest wind, at 3:30 a.m. Discovered by patrolman and reported at station and also at Oregon Inlet station. Keeper and crew hauled beach apparatus and surfboat abreast of vessel and awaited daylight before beginning action, as schooner was gradually working inshore, and in no immediate danger of going to pieces. As it grew light, it was found that surfboat could be used to advantage. This was soon launched, and the wreck reached. Crew of seven and their baggage were taken off and landed without mishap. The Oregon Inlet crew arrived in time to assist in landing and hauling surfboat upon beach. Sheltered crew at station for six days while engaged in saving stores, rigging, and sails of wrecked vessel. Master was cared for during fifteen days while this work was in progress, and was aided by station crew. Schooner was a total loss.

Wreck of schooner *E.S. Newman*, October 11, 1896:

Sails blown away and master obliged to beach her during hurricane 2 miles below station at 7 p.m. Signal of distress was immediately answered by patrolman's Coston light. Keeper and crew quickly started for the wreck with beach apparatus. The sea was sweeping over the beach and threatened to prevent reaching scene of disaster, but they finally gained a point near the wreck. It was found to be impossible to bury the sand anchor, as the tide was rushing over the entire beach, and they decided to tie a large-sized shot line around two surfmen and send them down through the surf as near the vessel as practicable. These men waded in and succeeded in throwing a line on board with the heaving stick. It was made fast to the master's three-year-old child who was then hauled off by the surfmen and carried ashore. In like manner his wife and the seven men composing the crew were rescued under great difficulties and with imminent peril to the lifesavers. They were taken to the station and furnished with food and clothing.

Wreck of the sloop *Lily Gay*, June 12, 1898:

Sprung a leak and sank in 3 feet of water in Pamlico sound, 2 miles from the station. Crew went out in supply boat and landed the baggage and stores, and at low water helped stop the leak and put the boat in trim. Sheltered the two men overnight, and next morning them and their effects on board the sloop.

Wrecks of the steamer *Marstenmoor*, January 28, 1900, and the schooner *Jane C. Harris*, February 25, 1900:

Marstenmoor - Stranded on New Inlet Shoal, some 600 yards offshore, shortly after midnight. Keeper called for assistance of Pea Island and Chicamacomico stations and took his beach apparatus abreast the vessel, it being too rough to use a boat. At daylight the three crews began operations with the wreck gun, and after great difficulty, owing to the distance and the strong current, succeeded in getting the gear set up. Master sent a note by the breeches buoy declining to land and asking that tugs be sent for. The keeper telephoned for tugs at daylight, and sent message to master to that effect, also urging him to land his crew, pending the arrival of help. Landed five men in the breeches buoy and then suspended operations, a tug having made her appearance.

Jane C. Harris - The Pea Island station is credited for having provided valuable assistance to the crew of Oregon Inlet. However the report contains a letter of acknowledgment from the master, mate and steward of the vessel: "We desire to compliment Captain M.W. Etheridge and his crew, and also the crew of the Pea Island Life-Saving Station, for their heroic efforts in rescuing us from the wreck of the schooner *Jane C. Harris*, under the most difficult circumstances, during a northwest gale and very cold, freezing weather. We were very kindly treated at the station after being taken off

African-American surfman from Pea Island Life-Saving Station. Cape Hatteras National Seashore

the wreck about nightfall by the lifesavers, who worked under the most trying conditions, and we thank them for all their noble work, which saved us from an untimely death."

Wreck of the schooner *Topaz*, April 14, 1903:

Capsized in a squall off Rollinson's Reef, 5 miles WNW of station, at 4 p.m. The lifesaving crew pulled to the vessel, but finding no one on board, returned to station. The next morning, accompanied by the surfmen from New Inlet station they assisted in righting, bailing out and temporarily repairing the capsized craft.

Wreck of the schooner *Montana*, December 11, 1904:

Shortly before midnight during a heavy NNW gale with thick snowstorm and rough sea the *Montana*, a three masted schooner laden with salt and carrying a crew of seven all told, struck the beach (north of the) station and 300 yards from shore. Heavy seas swept over her and the crew, after burning a torch for help, took refuge in the forerigging. The N. patrol promptly reported the disaster, and keeper and crew, provided with beach apparatus, reached the shore abreast of the wreck at 12:10 a.m., the keeper having telephoned for assistance to Oregon Inlet and New Inlet Stations, the former crew arriving at 1 a.m. and the latter some time later. It was impossible to launch a boat through the heavy surf, and after lighting a bonfire the life-savers placed the wreck gun and fired several lines, some of them going adrift and some to the wreck, but none in such a position that the shipwrecked crew could reach it. At daylight the surfmen laid a line over the spring stay which the crew succeeded in reaching, and after several hours of difficult work six men were landed. The seventh man, the ship's cook, being of advanced years, was washed overboard during the night and lost. Four of the rescued men were sheltered at the station for eleven days, and two for sixteen days. The *Montana* became a total wreck, and was sold by the master for a small sum.

Wreck of the schooner *Jennie Lockwood*, February 13, 1906:

During the severe northerly gale, thick weather and high sea this vessel stranded at 5 a.m. 200 yards E. of the former station. The patrol discovered her and reported her to the keeper, who telephoned to the Oregon Inlet station to come down and lend a hand at the wreck. At 10 a.m. the Pea Island crew

Pea Island in its later years as a lifeboat station. Cape Hatteras National Seashore

arrived abreast of the stranded craft with their beach apparatus and fired a shot line from the Lyle gun, the line falling over the forerigging. The crew from Oregon Inlet now arrived, and by means of the breeches buoy all hands – there were seven in all – were safely landed and taken to the Pea Island station and succored for six days. The schooner was lost.

Wreck of the *Charles J. Dumas*, December 11, 1911:

A letter of thanks from T.A. Curtis, master of the *Dumas*: "I desire to express my high appreciation of the faithful and energetic work performed by the keepers and crews of the New Inlet and Pea Island life-saving stations, under the most unfavorable circumstances, at the wreck of the schooner *Chas. J. Dumas*, December 27, 1911, on the North Carolina Coast. After being brought ashore were cared for hospitably until we were able to leave for Norfolk."

There is no doubt that some of the efforts of the Pea Island crew met with failure. But their successes were many. They were praised by the people they saved. Their efforts were recognized by the maritime industry and noted by the U.S. Life-Saving Service. The posthumous award of merit in 1996 from the U.S. Coast Guard recognizes years of courageous and dedicated service.

More research into the other individual stations of the U.S. Life-Saving Service is needed. The daily realities of the U.S. Life-Saving Service are little known to the general public. The stories of risk and heroes were not limited to Pea Island. But the story of Pea Island and other life-saving stations is worth investigating – not only as the history of the U.S. Life-Saving Service, but what the Life-Saving Service can tell us about American history and culture.

THE ISSUES
••• --- •• ••• --- •• ••• --- ••
Big Shoes To Fill
by John J. Galluzzo (Volume 5, Number 2)

ON March 17, 1902, disaster struck the United States Life-Saving Service, the news of which sent shockwaves from station to station and crossed the entire country.

Responding to a signal of distress from the stranded barge *Wadena*, Captain Marshall W. Eldredge called for his men to launch their surfboat from Massachusetts' Monomoy Life-Saving Station, on the "elbow" of Cape Cod. The lifesavers headed south, for Monomoy Point, picking up their keeper en route, who had marched out onto the beach to get a closer view of the wreck.

A heavy southeast wind battered the lifesavers in their boat, and the choppy seas made the trip no less difficult to bear. To the best of their estimation, though, due to the relatively stable condition of the barge resting on Shovelful Shoal, the rescue of the five stranded mariners aboard should not have been a precarious one.

When they reached the vessel, the lifesavers threw a heaving stick and line aboard, which the mariners then fastened on deck. One by one they shinnied down the rope, each more frantic and excited than the last. After the fifth man dropped into the surfboat, Captain Eldredge instructed his passengers to hunker down inside the boat, keep quiet and not move.

Just after pushing off from the *Wadena*, a tremendous wave slammed the lifesavers' craft, rousing the already terrified victims to an even higher state of fear. They reached up and grabbed for the surfmen, wrapping their arms around their necks, inhibiting their ability to row. Wave after wave continued to strike the surfboat until finally it overturned.

The crew succeeded in righting the boat twice before yet another huge wave blasted it upside-down again. By now the men from the *Wadena* had all succumbed to the sea, and the lifesavers were beginning to lose strength. Surfman Osborne Chase was the first to let go, and he was followed by Surfmen Valentine D. Nickerson and Edgar C. Small. The pounding waves washed over the lifesavers continuously, loosening any grip that they could get. Within moments Surfman Elijah Kendrick disappeared beneath the waves, and after him, Surfman Isaac T. Foy.

Captain Eldredge and Surfmen Seth Ellis and Arthur Rogers managed to hold on for a few moments longer, until one more blast knocked them all loose once again. Ellis and Rogers managed to orient themselves after being tossed about and re-established their grip, but their keeper could not. He grabbed onto a floating spar and drifted off into the distance, never again to be seen alive.

Rogers called out to Ellis across the boat to help him obtain a better grip. Unable to help his friend, Ellis assured him that they were drifting toward shore, and would be safe within minutes. Rogers, whose strength finally failed him, feebly said, "I have got to go," and slipped beneath the ocean's surface.

Still clinging to the overturned boat, Ellis stripped off his oil slicker, vest, and boots, and waited to see where the tide would take him. Within moments he passed by the stranded barge *Fitzpatrick*, also on Shovelful Shoal, but so enshrouded in fog and mist as to be impossible to be seen from the *Wadena*. Ellis watched as someone aboard the *Fitzpatrick*, he could not see who, tossed a fourteen foot dory over the side and into the water.

Just a few moments later, the dory appeared alongside Surfman Ellis, and a man he recognized as Elmer Mayo, a local wrecker, pulled him to safety in the boat. Mayo then struck out for shore, realizing that Ellis' strength was spent, and knowing full well that the crashing waves on the beach could mean their doom.

But Surfman Walter C. Bloomer, who had been left on shore to watch for the returning surfboat, spotted the incoming dory and rushed into the surf to help Mayo beach it. Safely ashore, Ellis totaled the dead: Captain Eldredge, six surfmen, and the five men from the *Wadena*.

Two days later, up the Massachusetts coast, Captain Joshua James of the Point Allerton Life-Saving Station in Hull had already heard the news of the tragedy when he ordered his men to launch their new Beebe-McClellan self-bailing, self-righting surfboat into the choppy Thursday morning waters off

Stony Beach. Unnerved by the untimely deaths of his lifesaving brethren, he determined that such a fate should never meet his crew, and so they began their unscheduled drill, at 7:00 AM, March 19, 1902, in a heavy northeast wind.

They practiced with the boat for an hour, with the 75-year old keeper at the steering oar. The Captain had made *Boston Globe* headlines just 11 months earlier when he passed his annual physical examination with better results than any of the twenty- or thirty-year olds under his command at the Point Allerton Station.

According to USLSS General Superintendent Sumner I. Kimball's 1909 biography of the keeper, "The drill was very satisfactory, and the Captain expressed his great gratification both with the behavior of the boat in freeing itself of the torrents of water which boarded it, and with the skill of the men. At length he gave the orders for landing, and when the boat grounded upon the beach opposite the station he sprang out upon the wet sand and, glancing at the sea a moment, he remarked to his men, 'The tide is ebbing.' These were his last words, but little did he know how true they were for him, for as he uttered them, he fell dead on the beach."

The sad and unexpected death of Captain Joshua James of the Point Allerton United States Life-Saving Service Station left a void not only in the hearts of the grieving townspeople, but atop the station's leadership as well.

James began his career as a volunteer lifesaver in December of 1841, less than a month after his fifteenth birthday; he became Hull's Massachusetts Humane Society boat keeper in 1876 at age 49; in 1889 he became the first keeper of the federal government's station at Point Allerton. Stories of his exploits during the Great Storm of November 25-26, 1888, the rescue of the crew of the stranded plaster-carrying schooner *Ulrica* on December 16, 1896, and his tireless efforts during the Portland Gale of 1898 earned national fame for the captain, his USLSS crews and local volunteers alike.

Now that he was gone, one question arose: who would replace Joshua James? To many Hullonians, the answer seemed simple. Francis Bernard Mitchell, James' great nephew (Mitchell's mother Marion was the daughter of the captain's older brother, Reinier) had served as a surfman at Point Allerton since the station's opening in March of 1890, beginning as the No. 5 man and moving up after 12 years to become the No. 1, the keeper's right hand man. He grew close to the captain, even writing out the daily reports as James in his later years dictated them.

Mitchell came from a large and heavily-decorated Hull lifesaving family. For their heroics during the Great Storm of 1888, Alonzo, Ambrose, Eugene,

Eugene, Jr., Harrison, Henry, John and William Mitchell all earned Humane Society bronze medals. The federal government responded by rewarding each man (except, for an unknown reason, Harrison) a silver lifesaving medal for the same deeds. In 1897, the Humane Society presented silver medals to Ambrose, Alonzo and Francis Mitchell for their roles in the *Ulrica* rescue.

James valued the skill and courage of the Mitchell men immensely and when the time came to select his first Life-Saving Service crew, he went as far as to enlist the aid of the local poet to push for the appointment of Francis' father Alonzo as the No. 1 surfman.

From a letter from John Boyle O'Reilly poet and editor of the Irish Catholic *Pilot*, to the Honorable Edward A. Moseley dated October 28, 1889: "Dear Ned: I want you to do me and the Hull public and humanity generally a great favor. (I am still living at Hull - in the new house.) Captain Joshua James, the chief of the new United States lifesaving crew at Hull, has not yet appointed his men. He told me last night that he wanted a first-class man as No. 1 of the crew, and that the best man in Hull, and one of the ablest surfmen on the whole coast, Alonzo Mitchell, was a year over the official age. I know Alonzo Mitchell, and he is all he says he is – a brave, powerful, cool-headed, experienced surfman; and a younger man than you or I.

"What I want you to do is ask Mr. (Sumner) Kimball to allow Capt. James to appoint Alonzo Mitchell. Capt. James is otherwise hampered in the restriction regarding relatives, for all our regular Hull fishermen are intermarried in the most extraordinary way. But this really ought to be allowed. It gives Capt. James as second the very best man in the town, his own selection, in whom he has complete confidence.

"Will you please urge this on Mr. Kimball, and let me know the result?" (James Jeffrey Roche, *Life of John Boyle O'Reilly*, 1891, p. 332.)

Yet neither O'Reilly nor James would ever see that desired result, as Kimball disallowed Mitchell's appointment. The superintendent had already given in to local pressure to disregard the age restriction once, when he allowed the appointment of James himself at sixty-two years old (the cutoff age being forty-five), and did not feel it necessary to do so again. Thirteen years later, Alonzo's son Francis had risen to the post of No. 1 surfman originally slated for his father.

Unfortunately for Francis, the service had undergone a major change in 1896 in regard to the appointment of keepers and surfmen, with the adoption of civil service rules. From its inception, the Life-Saving Service had always hired lifeboat crews locally, to allay fears among coastal residents of a heavy federal government influence on small communities. Over the years, though, too many politically-inspired postings of unskilled or otherwise untrustworthy men to paid positions of responsibility for the saving of lives from the sea forced the superintendent to reexamine the service's hiring and promotion policies. The civil service rules called for promotion to keeper to be based on merit on a district-wide basis, meaning that James' successor would be selected from the best surfmen working at all thirty-one stations along the Massachusetts coast, the Second Life-Saving District.

Opposition to the implementation of the civil service standards began early in Hull. Local newspaper editor David Porter Mathews of the *Hull Beacon*, a nephew of Joshua James, spoke out against it in a somewhat parochial fashion following the Portland Gale of 1898, in his December 10, 1898 article, "Hull Life Savers Have No Peers": "We do not pretend to assert that the civil service produces no efficient lifesavers, but we greatly doubt that, on the average, it is able, even by its strict examinations, to furnish as good men as can be picked from the Volunteers of Hull or any of our coast-wise towns.

"It is a fact which cannot be denied that the augmentation of the United States crew by the Volunteers made the efforts to save the lives of shipwrecked sailors last week entirely possible.

"The regular lifesavers are good, reliable men, nevertheless, the volunteers have no peers in the work. Captain James was for many years a volunteer life-saver, and as such made his world-wide reputation long before the regular service was instituted here. It is his great experience as a volunteer that now makes his services so valuable to the government.

"When new men are needed on the station they should be selected from the men living here, men who understand the business thoroughly. In fact they are veterans with a knowledge of lifesaving that novices could not attain to until after many years of service."

While awaiting official word, Francis Mitchell remained on as acting keeper for the next three months after James' death. On June 8, 1902, after the regular surfmen had gone home for the summer, he and a volunteer rescued eight people from a drifting sailboat, transporting them back to the station.

Somehow, though, Mitchell had incurred the dislike of the station's next door neighbor, local newspaper publisher Floretta Vining. From the windows of her Vining Villa, Vining, who had donated the land on which the government built Point Allerton station and who therefore believed she could

Vining Villa overshadowed the Point Allerton station, two doors down on the right. The shadow of its prime occupant, local newspaper editor Floretta Vining, loomed over the station as well. Hull Historical Society

expect its tenants to live up to her moral standards, watched over the life-savers on a daily basis.

The sole heiress to a magnificent fortune acquired by her father Alexander's years in the leather goods and hotel management trades, Vining owned most of the property on Stony Beach, the location of the Point Allerton station. Years earlier she had donated the land on which the Massachusetts Humane Society built its Stony Beach lifeboat and mortar stations. Yet for all her philanthropy and hard work for the social betterment of the town she called her summer home, Vining alienated many potential allies through her venomous editorials, printed weekly through the nine newspapers in her South Shore Syndicate.

Occasionally, unsuspecting bystanders became targeted victims of her poison quill, such as 24-year veteran lifesaver Captain Samuel O. Fisher and the surfmen of the Race Point Life-Saving Station on Cape Cod. Vining unleashed her wrath on them in her August 28, 1903 *Hull Beacon* editorial, "My trip to Provincetown"; "It was 12 o'clock when we finished our drive and the last part of it was on the state road to the lifesaving station in charge of Capt. Fisher. We were obliged to leave the carriage and walk to the station. I have seen sand but never in my life did I ever walk through any such deep sand as I did there.

"Those lazy men will walk through that sand many times daily before they will build a walk with all the wood and timber that washes in from the ocean. The government furnishes nails and yet these men sit and look at one another day in and day out for they do no work. I have visited lifesaving stations all over the country but I never saw one so poorly kept as Race Point off Provincetown. I live next door to a station and know whereof I speak. The station is an old one I know, but the things I speak of are poor management and the want of thrift.

"The boat house and boats were all in confusion, thrown down anywhere. The paraphernalia used was all in confusion, every floor in the house was worn into the wood for the want of oil and varnish which the government in quantities furnish. The back door is used for a front door and there was a half hogshead filled with swill and broken crockery. This station has two luxuries, a cook and a team, and may it be said of the cook her place was neat and clean and she was neatly dressed. The neglect of the establishment as a whole is the keeper's fault, he cannot have control over his men. I openly say it was the worst looking and dirtiest station I was ever in and others of the party in authority were of my opinion. Were I the keeper of Race Point I would varnish and paint it and build a walk through sand two feet deep rather than wade through it.

"I think Mr. Kimball should pay that station a visit. I know what I am talking about. I have given a good deal of time to understand the lifesaving business and know what the government furnishes to the keepers."

Vining also understood the value of the presence of the lifesavers themselves so near to her home, but never shied away from confronting them when she felt it necessary. "Judge Knowlton, in the Suffolk supreme court, Wednesday, gave a hearing on the bill in equity brought by Mr. Thomas H. Leavitt and Floretta Vining against James H. Murphy of the Stony Beach Life-Saving Station at Hull, and also the bill in equity brought by Murphy against Thomas Leavitt, et al. The bill brought against Murphy asks the court to enforce against him the restrictions contained in his deed of the lot of land at Hull, upon which his home is built, claiming that he has violated them by building a house costing less than $800, and by placing it nearer than 10 feet from the street. They ask that he be ordered to remove the house altogether, or to alter it to conform to the restrictions. His house stands opposite the life-saving station. Murphy claims the real plaintiff is Miss Vining, who has a cottage a short distance from his, on the opposite side of the street, and that she has no title to her land from the trustees of the Nantasket Company, who owned his land and contiguous lots some years ago, and inserted the restrictions, and therefore has no right to object. He further says that the proper parties to object, having knowledge of the facts when he was building his house, did not then object to the manner in which he built, and that he should not

The irrepressible Floretta Vining campaigned against the appointment of Francis Bernard Mitchell as keeper of the Point Allerton Life-Saving Station in 1902. Hull Historical Society

be obliged now to remove or to alter the building." ("Life Saver's Little House. Claim Made That He Has Violated the Restriction Contained In His Deed," *Hull Beacon*, May 8, 1897). A month later the paper reported that Murphy had won the court battle, and was allowed to keep his home.

Silently, in the spring of 1902, Floretta Vining began her campaign against Francis Mitchell's promotion to keeper of the Point Allerton station.

The week of July 4, 1902, District Superintendent Benjamin C. Sparrow appointed the new Point Allerton keeper from his office in Orleans, Massachusetts, after reviewing the records of all the Massachusetts surfmen. Sparrow had also recently spent time searching for a new crew to serve under new Keeper Seth Ellis of the Monomoy Station. One Hull man, Stillman Dexter Mitchell, a temporary surfman who filled in at the Point Allerton station the day that James died, drew a full-time position at Monomoy.

Sparrow's choice for the new keeper, William Sparrow of Provincetown, raised eyebrows in Hull. Although they shared no relation, their common surname sparked immediate grumbling of nepotism throughout the town. And, as only a five-year veteran of the Life-Saving Service, beginning his career as the No. 1 surfman at the new Wood End (Provincetown) station in 1897, William Sparrow could not claim nearly as much experience as either Francis Mitchell or James Murphy, also a long-time Point Allerton surfman. Mitchell, angered by Sparrow's appointment and Vining's apparent meddling, left the service.

Vining, triumphant, gloated through her weekly *Hull Beacon* notes column of July 4. "All Hull combined and many others, besides many steamboat companies for the appointment of a certain man to be made captain of the Point Allerton Life-Saving Station. Miss Vining alone objected and her wishes were conceded to."

One week later, though, Vining paid dearly for her interventionist tactics. "Yes, I objected to Francis Mitchell's appointment as captain for the Life-Saving Station. It is far better that another should hold the very responsible position, for many reasons. A life-saving station should be maintained for the business for which it is formed and is not a place for visitors.

"Since Mr. Sparrow arrived, my beautiful and faithful dog Bruno has been poisoned. That there lives within the borders of this town so contemptible and despicable a wretch as to visit their miserable vengeance for imagining injuries upon an innocent dumb animal, to retaliate upon its mistress, is more than decent people can understand." (*Hull Beacon*, July 11, 1902.) Vining assumed that Mitchell had poisoned her dog.

For the rest of the summer, Vining watched out her windows as Keeper Sparrow's industrious attitude and work ethic helped him win over the hearts of the townspeople, reporting finally on August 29th, "The new lifesaving captain is very much liked by everybody." She also took whatever chances she could to report on the misdeeds of Francis Mitchell, who gave her ample opportunity to do so. Knowing full well that she held a particular dislike for the poor fishermen who set up shacks on Stony Beach, which she considered eyesores in an otherwise beautiful community, Mitchell spent time amongst them, across the way from Vining Villa. "Last Saturday night Dutch Charlie returned from a week's outing to his floating shanty and several of his neighbors helped him celebrate the event. Among them were Andrew Pope, John Saunderson and Francis B. Mitchell. The hour 1:30 a.m. It will be remembered that Mr. Mitchell was the aspirant for captain of the life-saving station. The noise was such that the lifesavers went over to investigate and Francis Mitchell used his billy over the head and shoulders of the lifesavers." (*Hull Beacon*, September 26, 1902.)

By January of 1903, Floretta would report that she had made firewood of the shanties on the beach, but by that time her feud with Mitchell had ended, at least publicly. Captain Sparrow served at Point Allerton for the next eighteen years, as the station's only USLSS keeper other than Joshua James, and its first U.S. Coast Guard commanding officer. Vining continued to editorialize weekly and to stick her nose in where it was not necessarily wanted, while Francis Mitchell went on to a distinguished career with the Hull police force. After his death in 1934, the town memorialized him by printing his picture in the opening pages of the Town of Hull Annual Report, a privilege reserved for only its most revered citizens: "His brave deeds as a lifesaver were many, and his later service as a police officer was continually faithful and efficient. The quiet geniality of his friendly personality will long be remembered by his many friends in this, the town of his birth." His feud with Vining proved to be an aberration in an otherwise fine career in public service.

It took almost a year, but finally when he realized that his beloved Hull shoreline was being watched over by able and willing hands, Joshua James could rest in peace.

THE ISSUES

•••------••• •••------••• •••------•••

The Tragedy of Motor Lifeboat No. 36542

by Dewey Livingston (Volume 4, Number 3)

OF the 36-foot motor lifeboats that served Point Reyes Lifeboat Station in California, *No. 36542* figured prominently as one of the active boats for almost a decade and for its role in the station's greatest tragedy. The U.S. Coast Guard opened the Point Reyes Lifeboat Station in 1927 as a replacement for its 1890 Life-Saving Station, moving the location from the treacherous Great Beach to a protected spot in Drake's Bay. Motor Lifeboat *No. 36542*, built in 1953 at the Coast Guard boatyard at Curtis Bay Maryland, arrived at Point Reyes around 1954 after serving a short time at Arena Cove Lifeboat Station.

On a cold Thanksgiving Eve in 1960, two Point Reyes crewmen answered a routine call to aid a fishing boat near Bodega Bay, about 24 miles from the station. After securing the civilian vessel in her port, Boatswain's Mate First Class Anthony R. Holmes and 19 year-old Enginemen Fireman Hugh James McClement radioed the lifeboat station that they would be returning to Point Reyes in less than an hour.

When the boat did not appear on schedule and the crew did not respond to radio calls, other crewmen at the station became concerned and a search ensued. About 9 a.m. the next morning, *36542* was found aground on Great Beach between the RCA receiving station and Point Reyes Lighthouse, nose to shore with propellers turning and no one aboard.

Coast Guardsmen, sheriff's deputies, and some 40 local volunteers searched the beaches for many days following; a Coast Guard helicopter, seaplanes and two 95-foot patrol boats backed up the effort. The locals, mostly dairy ranchers (many of the "farmer's daughters" were favorites with

Ill-fated Coast Guard motor lifeboat 36542 *on a calm day in Drake's Bay, Point Reyes, California.* National Park Service

the young surfmen in this isolated station), had enjoyed a 70-year relationship with the Life-Saving Service and Coast Guard and took the task to heart.

Although hopes of finding the men alive faded over the weekend, the search was extended at the urging of young McClement's mother. One afternoon, five days after the empty boat was discovered, the body of Holmes was spotted by a helicopter patrol and retrieved on the beach near the Spaletta dairy ranch. On December 16, some three weeks after the incident, searchers found McClement's body.

The motor lifeboat, made to right itself if knocked over, no doubt threw the untethered men into heavy seas and continued pilotless to the beach. Disoriented by the darkness and cold in the notorious Pacific Coast surf of Point Reyes, the men probably didn't have much a chance of survival.

The boat was repaired and back in service early the next year, but held a grim reputation with some of the men for years after. Officer-in-Charge Jim Crunk recalled that his men, himself included, tried not to consider the boat to be haunted but couldn't shake the memory of the tragedy. *No. 36542* was transferred to the newly-built Coast Guard Station Bodega Bay in 1963. There the men held the boat in high esteem.

Motor Lifeboat *No. 36542* remained in service at Bodega Bay for about thirteen years, after which she was transferred for short stints at Yerba Buena Island and Fort Point in San Francisco Bay. She spent the end of her career at Eureka's Humboldt Bay Lifeboat Station as the last 36-foot motor lifeboat in service in the 12th Coast Guard District.

When the Coast Guard surveyed *36542* as surplus in 1982, Point Reyes National Lakeshore acquired her as an artifact to grace the former lifeboat station, which had been disestablished on December 16, 1968 and transferred to the park. In 1990, the Point Reyes Lifeboat Station, including Motor Lifeboat *No. 36542*, was designated a National Historic Landmark. The rehabilitated station acts as an education center, with the ill-fated motor lifeboat preserved as the main historical attraction, sitting on a steel cradle on the rare intact marine railway. Unfortunately, the historic station is seldom open to the public. Park staff plans to increase interpretation of the station some time in the future.

THE RESCUES

The Gold Medal Shipwreck

by Frederick Stonehouse (Volume 1, Number 1)

MOST of the rescues performed by the old lifesavers and later the early Coast Guard were "reasonably routine." The storm conditions may have been truly horrible and the courage and bravery of the crews beyond comparison, but at least all of the equipment usually worked and all of the surfmen were healthy. This was not the case in the wreck of the steamer *H.B. Runnels*.

During the early morning hours of November 14, 1919, a wild northwest storm boiled over Lake Superior. Mountainous seas marched across the horizon and a wind born in the depths of an arctic hell swept across the lonely shore. A blizzard blotted out the world and temperatures plummeted to the low teens. Everywhere vessels battled against the ravages of the storm. One was the 178-foot, 889-ton wooden steamer *H.B. Runnels*, upbound with coal for Lake Linden on the Keweenaw Peninsula in Michigan.

The *Runnels'* adventure began at 5:30 a.m. when surfman George Olson, on watch at the Grand Marais, Michigan, Coast Guard Station lookout tower, reported a steamer on the wrong side of the west pier at the harbor entrance. Apparently she was trying to shelter in the bay. Thinking that if she wasn't yet in trouble, she soon would be, he alertly rang the alarm. The station crew quickly responded by preparing the beach apparatus, then launching the 34-foot motor lifeboat. The boathouse was in the sheltered harbor, so the lifeboat was safe in calm water.

The steamer, however, was seen to back out into the lake and apparently hove to, about a mile and a half to the north of the station. Since the steamer showed no distress signals, the Coast Guard assumed she would wait until daylight to try to enter the harbor, rather than chance it in the dark. But in any case, they would be prepared.

Number one surfman A.E. Kristofferson was left in charge of the station in the absence due to illness of the keeper, Benjamin Trudell. Captain of the station since it opened in 1900, Trudell was a veteran of many rescues and a living legend along the south shore of Superior. His long experience, local knowledge and steady leadership was an important ingredient in the station's success. The 50-mile expanse of desolate Lake Superior shore between Whitefish Point and Grand Marais has long been known as the "Shipwreck Coast." At least 75 vessels have met tragedy along this forbidding shore. If the dark forest could talk, what terrible tales it could tell!

After quickly assessing the situation, in the event rescue was needed, Kristofferson went over to Coast Guard sub-chaser *438* which was sheltering in the harbor. The *438* had been en route to Grand Marais, Minnesota, to close down the station there for the winter when the storm struck, forcing her to duck into the safety of the harbor. The 110-foot sub-chaser was one of 440 vessels completed for World War I Coast Guard service. The *438*, which later became the USCG *Cook*, stayed in service until 1936 when she was sold to private interests only to reenter Coast Guard service for World War II in 1943. She was decommissioned in 1945. Her normal complement was one officer and 24 enlisted sailors. Kristofferson asked the *438's* captain, G.R.

The Laker H.B. Runnels *before her loss on Lake Superior in 1919. Frederick Stonehouse and Rutherford B. Hayes Library*

O'Connor, for help. Several of the station's surfmen were sick and extra men would be needed to help haul the McClellan surfboat through the snow to the wreck site.

O'Connor agreed to provide whatever assistance he could, but he also told Kristofferson that he had aboard as a guest, John O. Anderson, the veteran keeper of the Chicago Life-Saving Station. Could he help if a rescue was called for? Eagerly, Kristofferson accepted the offer.

As Kristofferson and Anderson were walking back to the station, they saw that the steamer had drifted close ashore on the wrong side of the pier and was now sounding distress signals. Visibility was terrible, but both could make her out as the *Runnels*. The *Runnels* had sheltered in Grand Marais early on November 13 from the storm. When the weather improved about midnight she left to continue her trip. Just after rounding Au Sable Point, about eight miles out, she was slammed by the renewed tempest. Instead of trying to battle her way through to Lake Linden, a run of 115 miles before reaching the safety of the Portage Lake Ship Canal, she headed back for Grand Marais. About 5:30 a.m., Captain Hugh O'Hagan cautiously approached the entry from upwind. When he thought he had correctly gauged the wind and wave conditions, he rang for full speed. With the wind on the stern quarter and a wicked cross sea slicing past his counter, he would need both speed and luck to make it in between the piers. One or the other, or both, failed him. Driven by wind and sea, he started to drift down on the east pier. In a doomed effort to save himself, he attempted to back out to a safe distance to try again. Unable to stand up to the force of the waves crashing into the stern, the steering gear failed and the *Runnels* was left to the mercy of the unforgiving lake. The crew jury-rigged tackle on the tiller, but under the terrible force of the swinging rudder, it was torn loose.

When Kristofferson and Anderson reached the station they discovered the motor lifeboat was disabled. After the lookout spotted the *Runnels* close in and blowing distress signals, the station crew had started off in the boat intending to pick up Kristofferson and additional help at the *438*. But the engine stalled en route and unable to repair it, the men had to anchor and wade ashore. For this rescue the lifeboat was out of action. Plan A was out; on to plan B.

Under the direction of the keeper and number one surfman, the Coast Guardsmen, assisted by the Grand Marais lightkeeper, part of the *438* crew and local volunteers, hauled the apparatus cart and surfboat through the blizzard to the beach opposite the *Runnels*. The dying steamer stood a long five hundred to six hundred yards out, hard on a sand bar. Her whistle continued to sound mournful moans of distress.

Forced broadside to the waves, the steamer was assaulted without mercy. Sea after sea smashed into her, each putting another nail into her coffin. Everything above water was coated in a thick coat of ice. It would be only a matter of time before she went to pieces and her seventeen-man crew drowned in the crashing waves.

As made second nature by years of drill, the station crew quickly set up the beach apparatus and charged the Lyle gun with a six full ounces of Hazard's powder. After carefully aiming the gun, Anderson grasped the lanyard firmly in one hand and waited. He held his fire until just the right moment, when the icy blasts paused and then cut loose. The projectile fired cleanly, the shot line uncoiling neatly behind. The thin line draped across the bow. Under the terrible weather conditions, it was a tremendous shot. It was also a shot that had to be made, since the bow was the only area not either under water or being regularly swept by the waves.

Quickly the *Runnels* crew hauled away at the shot line and brought the block with the whip aboard. This was secured to the post of the steering wheel in the pilothouse. It was the only object still standing strong enough to serve as an anchor point.

Because the *Runnels* was laying broadside to the waves, a vicious cross sea and current was set on the lee side, that side of the vessel facing the shore. The whip was caught in the cross current and kept turning the whip block and line, which in turn fouled. Considering the shore ends of the whip were set approximately 300 feet apart, to prevent this very problem, its occurrence was remarkable. Unable to pull the heavy hawser necessary to support the breeches buoy through the fouled block, any attempt to use the breeches buoy was finished. Plan B was out, on to plan C.

The Coast Guardsmen brought both ends of the whip tightly together to form a single double line and tied it off to the bow shackle. When the shore ends of the whip were made fast to the sand anchor, the whip could be used as a guideline for the surfboat. Regardless of what the waves and current did, the surfboat could travel a direct course between the beach and wreck. Backing the wagon as far into the waves as they dared, the crew launched the surfboat.

With Anderson at the steering oar, the surfboat headed through the breakers and onto the wreck. It was a hellish trip. Several times grasping waves swept men completely out of the boat. Each time they climbed back

The Grand Marais Life-Saving Station on Lake Superior. Surfmen went out from this station to the Runnels *rescue. Michigan State Archives*

aboard and continued to pull for the *Runnels*. Stinging spray froze on their faces while numbed fingers and hands fought to hold onto the heavy oars. Their arms felt like lead. Reaching the wreck they found the waves too high to even come alongside. The shipwrecked sailors had to slide down the rope from the ship hand over hand and into the boat. On the first trip they managed to land four of the *Runnels'* men. They seemed half dead from exposure.

In total four trips were made through the boiling surf and all seventeen sailors were rescued. The last run was the worst. Instead of the eight rowers normally used, only six men were available. All others were either injured or too exhausted to be efficient. Once the short-handed crew reached the wreck, they had the special problem of getting the last two crewmen aboard, Captain Hugh O'Hagan and chief engineer, Joseph Hemmeth. Since both were elderly a heaving line was thrown aboard and fastened around each man.

It was intended that the men would slide down the whip as the others had done. But both the captain and engineer, utterly fatigued and stiff with cold, dropped off short, landing in the water. Each in turn had to be hauled to the boat and manhandled aboard. In the case of the engineer, who weighed 315 pounds, it was backbreaking work.

From the official records, only Anderson, Kristofferson and Surfman Russe Martin had the stamina to make all four trips, and that stamina was indeed remarkable. Anderson was washed out of the boat three times and Kristofferson at least twice. True to their performance, they kept coming back for more, after all, regulations said they had to go out. They didn't say anything about coming back.

On the first trip the boat was manned with station men, volunteers from the *438* and a local fisherman. When they returned to the beach, three of the crewmen were all in. Taken with cramps from the immersion in the cold water and tremendous exertion, they had to be carried away. Two of the fishermen, the Graham brothers, Christopher and Joseph, were former lifesavers and knew the drills well. As the crewmen succumbed, volunteers readily took their places. There were lives to be saved and it was not the place nor time for the faint-hearted.

For the wives of both the station crew and fishermen it must have been an especially difficult time, but they bore their fear well. A local observer reported that there was no "whimpering among the wives of the fishermen who stood on shore and waved encouragement to their menfolk."

The last surfboat reached the *Runnels* at 12:40 in the afternoon. Thirty minutes later the steamer broke up completely. The rescue was made just in the nick of time.

The physical abuse suffered by the boat crew was terrible. When they were finally finished, their frozen lifejackets and clothing had to be cut off.

Although Captain O'Connor was the senior Coast Guard officer present, he wisely left the rescue to the experts, Anderson and Kristofferson. But after the final trip, when he saw how utterly fatigued the trusty number one surfman was, he relieved him of all responsibilities for the beach apparatus and related equipment and from any station duties and ordered him to bed. This was an extraordinary action on the part of O'Connor since the careful accountability and maintenance of equipment immediately after a rescue was a hallmark of the old lifesaving crews.

No beach patrols were run that night. The men were too ill or too spent. O'Connor also left one of his crew to nurse Surfman Glen Wells. Recently returned from the hospital after a serious operation, he nonetheless did his duty the best he could. After the first desperate trip through the breakers he had to be carried from the boat and back to the station. A local physician was kept busy not only with Wells, but also other sick or injured surfmen and survivors. The station also provided 29 meals to the *Runnels* crew and men from the *438*. Relief clothing was issued to the victims who lost everything when the steamer broke up.

On November 16, Keeper Trudell returned from leave and after learning of the desperate work of the previous day, began to put things back to order. Still short-handed because of sick surfmen, several local men were hired to clean and recover the equipment, repair the broken motor lifeboat and generally prepare the station for action, should action again be needed.

The *Runnels* rescue demonstrated the indomitable spirit and resourcefulness of the old lifesaving crews. It had only been four years since the Life-Saving Service was combined with the Revenue Marine to form the fledgling Coast Guard and its strong backbone was still very much in evidence. When a plan went awry, another was rapidly developed. In spite of the sickness of the crewmen, they toughed it through. When necessary, volunteers were used. If the keeper was absent, it was no problem. The number one surfman took charge and accomplished the mission.

As a tribute to their bravery, a gold lifesaving medal was awarded to each man, including Anderson and the four Grand Marais fishermen.

The *Runnels* had also seen salt-water duty. In October of 1898, she, together with a fleet of 40 other lake craft, had been sent to the eastern seaboard to mitigate vessel shortages caused by the Spanish American War. For several months she ran out of Eastport, Maine. In the spring of 1899 she had returned to the lakes.

She was also no stranger to Lake Superior shipwreck. On May 29, 1895, her cargo of coal had caught fire when she was on Lake Erie. To extinguish it, she was scuttled in shallow water. On November 27, 1897, she had stranded during a snowstorm on Point Abbaye at the entrance of Huron Bay. She was released with $5,000 in damages. In the 1919 wreck, the *Runnels* was a total loss of $60,000.

THE RESCUES
Brave Men of Hull

by Robert W. Haley (Volume 1, Number 4)

HULL, Massachusetts, is a long, narrow peninsula seven miles in length and shaped like the number seven. Born of the last ice age, composed mainly of drumlins and a barrier beach, it completes the outer southeastern edge of Boston Harbor. Until about 1905, shipping came and left Boston Harbor by way of Hull via Nantasket Roads, a relatively narrow and dangerous channel. The channel entrance lies between Boston Light, on Little Brewster Island, and Point Allerton, on the northern edge of the Hull peninsula. Shore-based lifesaving began early and was needed frequently off Hull.

After it was established in 1786, the Massachusetts Humane Society placed one of its first huts of refuge on Nantasket Beach in Hull. Organized and effective lifesaving was first recorded here in 1841, when Humane Society volunteers saved five crewmembers from the ship *Emeline*, and twelve from the wreck of the *Mohawk*. By 1845 using the surfboat stationed there, Massachusetts Humane Society crews had saved thirty-six lives. Volunteer lifesaving increased markedly in Hull during the next forty years with five lifeboat/surfboat stations and a mortar station active along this small stretch of coast. In the great storm of November 1888, Massachusetts Humane Society volunteers under Captain Joshua James saved twenty-nine persons from six wrecks during a two-day period. The U.S. Life-Saving Service awarded these volunteers eleven gold and four silver lifesaving medals for their heroic efforts.

Joshua James first became a Massachusetts Humane Society volunteer in 1844, and was keeper of the six Hull stations from around 1876 to 1889. In 1889, the federal government constructed a new U.S. Life-Saving Service

Station at Hull. There was no finer surfman in the region and at age 62, and with a special waiver granted by the U.S. Life-Saving Service, Joshua James became the first Keeper of the new Point Allerton Life-Saving Station.[1]

It was while serving as keeper of Point Allerton Life-Saving Station that Joshua James faced one of his greatest challenges. During the night of December 15, 1896, a severe northeast storm, with gale force winds and heavy snow, began to hit the Massachusetts coast. Off Cape Cod, the three-masted schooner *Ulrica*, of British registry, bound from Parrsboro, Nova Scotia to Hoboken, New Jersey with a cargo of plaster, was caught in the intensifying storm. The seven-man crew headed the ship for Boston Harbor. During the next few hours, wind gusts destroyed her sails, and she was forced to drop both her anchors. Shortly the ship began to drag her anchors, grounding in the breakers off Nantasket Beach about 8 a.m. on December 16. Her ghostly white hull was spotted by the south patrolman of the Point Allerton Station, and he hurried back to the station to report the wreck. The lifesaving crew had already been notified by telephone of the schooner's plight, and Captain James accepted the offer of the railroad, which ran nearby to carry the crew to the wreck site, about two and a half miles south-east of the station. One surfman was left to obtain horses and bring the beach cart to the disaster scene.

On arrival, the lifesavers promptly brought the Massachusetts Humane Society's large lifeboat, *Nantasket*, housed nearby, to the beach opposite the ship. Captain James found very heavy seas breaking over the *Ulrica*, sweeping across her at all points forward of the mizzenmast. The ship's crew was huddled on the ship's after-house, and in the mizzen rigging. He felt that they were in great peril, "and dared not wait for our beach apparatus to arrive." Taking his own crew of seven, and six Humane Society volunteers, he quickly had the big green lifeboat launched. Twice the waves hurled her back to the beach. The third time they succeeded in getting off, but could make only slow progress toward the *Ulrica* because of the strong current running along the shore. When halfway there, a "towering" sea struck *Nantasket*, driving her astern, and tipping her to a near vertical position. Keeper Joshua James was thrown upward and backward out of the boat by the force of the wave on his steering oar, or by its blade striking the bottom. As the boat passed him, he caught hold of a surfman's oar, and was dragged back to the beach with the lifeboat. One newspaper account states, "the doughty veteran was not lost' but "danced out of the cauldron laughing gaily although soaked to the skin." A more reasonable account says that the captain

December, 1896. Salvage crew working on Ulrica *on a calm winter's day.* Hull *Historical Society*

splashed his way shoreward, soaked and shivering." The latter seems better descriptive of a seventy-year-old man, thrown into icy water, and emerging into the dubious comfort of a northeast snowstorm.

Meanwhile, the beach apparatus had arrived. "The sea was making a breach across her from her mizzenmast forward." Captain James then fired two shots across the *Ulrica* with the Lyle gun, but the frozen crew made no attempt to get either line. The third shot fell across the rigging toplift, and slid down to where the crew could retrieve it. The whip line and the hawser were hauled off slowly, for only part of the ship's crew was now capable of helping. Then, because of their exhausted state, they were unable to make fast either line very high in the mizzen rigging. Captain James thought it was too dangerous, under these conditions, to attempt to use the breeches buoy for their rescue, fearing that the whip line would foul the hawser. (There is an account describing his attempt to have the lines stretched over the roof of a nearby house, hoping to elevate them out of the water. If true, the attempt was obviously unsuccessful.) Joshua James then decided to make another attempt to use the lifeboat.

This time, the lifesavers took five Massachusetts Humane Society volunteers with them. They attached the lifeboat to the hawser, presumably to the traveler block (pulley), and fastened another line to her stern. Captain James did not provide an exact description of the maneuvers used. He wrote that "by hauling on the hawser and by the use of the oars," aided by the men controlling the stern line from shore, they managed to work the lifeboat out to the side of the *Ulrica.*

Keeper James also stated that they were "obliged to encounter some very heavy broad side seas" as they went. Dennis R. Means, a direct descendant of the captain, who has written an excellent history of the *Nantasket* in *The American Neptune*, furnishes other information as to the procedure. He writes that "the hawser served to guide a James' Trolley," and that "its car was *Nantasket.*" The men on shore, holding the stern line, acted as a "human rudder." From Captain James' account, it appears that some men aboard *Nantasket* hauled the big lifeboat hand over hand along the hawser, while others rowed. The keeper left no description of the obvious difficulty, discomfort, and danger in doing this.[2]

Then, Captain James wrote simply, that they "were very fortunate in getting all the crew, and landing safely." A contemporary account, however, suggests that the lifesavers had to board the vessel themselves. The survivors were taken to a nearby hotel, the Seafoam House, where they were stabilized for several hours before being returned to the station. "Old Ocean, in her maddest mood, raged over this failure of human sacrifice, and to console herself, gulped down the carcass of a poor wrecked ship. The prey sought for so fiercely had been snatched into safety. Again, science, skill, bravery and hardihood had made man master of the waters."[3]

Old Ocean, however, had one last surprise for the lifesavers. On January 8, 1897, a crew of ten salvage workers were aboard *Ulrica.* Disregarding increasing northeast winds and roughening seas, they remained aboard until conditions prevented them from returning safely to shore in their own boat. Anticipating this problem, Captain James and his surfmen had gone to the wreck site, and promptly launched a small, older Humane Society surfboat. Being struck by "two bad seas" on the way out, the boat began to leak rapidly. Half full of water, and with two men bailing constantly, the surfboat returned to shore. Then rolling out faithful, big *Nantasket*, the lifesavers, accompanied by two Humane Society volunteers, returned to *Ulrica*, and successfully removed the salvage crew.

So ended the story of *Ulrica*, an unfortunate ship, with a most fortunate crew. The *Boston Globe* headline of December 17, 1896, described the actions of the lifesavers simply and well: "Brave Men of Hull."

THE RESCUES
An Incident at a Life-Saving Station
by Dennis L. Noble (Volume 1, Number 2)

MUCH of the daily work of those who served in the U.S. Life-Saving Service was routine. There was nothing like a lookout tower watch, for instance, to create crushing boredom. Furthermore, the Life-Saving Service regulations stated that a surfman had to stand during these watches and so boredom was combined with tired feet. The lifesavers could never tell, however, when boredom would suddenly turn into adrenaline-pumping terror. An incident on November 19, 1908, at Waadaah Island Life-Saving Station illustrates the dangers crews faced. Waadaah Island is a small wooded island off Neah Bay, Washington, at the northwest tip of the Olympic Peninsula. In 1908 Waadaah Island was a new station, recently built to replace the original Neah Bay station that had been discontinued earlier. For some years the area had been without a lifesaving station, but now had a new station complete with a motor lifeboat.

At 9:00 a.m. that winter day the Waadaah Island crew set out to test their new power lifeboat. Keeper George W. McAfee and eight surfmen pushed off from the station, leaving surfman George Heise behind to oversee the station during their trial run. Keeper McAfee set course eastward in the Strait of Juan de Fuca to Clallam Bay, about twenty miles distance. The lifeboat towed a dory during the journey. As is common in this region, as the crew began their run it was raining and there was a light southeast wind. The crew ate at the community of Clallam Bay and then began their run back to the station.

On the return trip, the wind rose and shifted to the southwest and started to build up the waves in the strait. The lifeboat arrived off the launchway in the dark and sounded a whistle to let Surfman Heise know they had arrived

This view of Waadaah Island shows the life-saving station at center. The island is located in the northwest corner of the state of Washington. Landing here could be treacherous in the heavy Pacific surf. United States Coast Guard Academy

and to bring down a lantern to help guide them onto the boat ramp. To understand what happened next, picture in your mind the launchway ran between them. Heavy seas can make landing a boat here dangerous and Keeper McAfee noted that during periods of bad weather a swirl developed at the entrance to the reefs.

Because of the rough conditions, Keeper McAfee decided he would not try to land the motor lifeboat, but would try to anchor in a protected area and wait until daylight and perhaps better weather. George McAfee let five of his surfmen take the dory into the station, while he and three others would stay with the lifeboat.

Surfman Fritz Klintberg and August Mullick took the oars and pulled toward the light held by Heise, who was standing on the boat ramp. The boat approached the dangerous area between the two reefs as a sudden squall swept down the straits. As the boat was worked in between the reefs, surfman Klintberg's oar broke. This caused the dory to swing sideways and, in what seemed like an instantaneous moment, the small dory slammed into the reef, capsized and the five surfmen were thrown into the cold water of the straits.

In the flickering light of his lantern, Heise saw the dory "strike the rocks like a shot" then swing around and turn over. The surfmen in the boat struggled to reach safety. Surfman Heise quickly picked his way over the rocks, helping Surfman Alfred Rimer out of the water. Heise saw that Klintberg was safely on the rocks and did not appear injured. He yelled for Klintberg to run to the station for more lanterns. Klintberg also picked up a megaphone and shouted to Keeper McAfee about the accident. A quick muster revealed that Surfman John Jacobsen and John Sundstrom were recovered.

The tragic story of Waadaah Island Life-Saving Station's two lost surfmen would normally end after the USLSS investigation and the men simply added to the statistics of the U.S. Life-Saving Service. There is, however, an interesting epilogue to the incident. To understand the epilogue, readers should be aware of the modern day setting of Neah Bay, Washington.

The present day Neah Bay Coast Guard Station is a modern brick structure sitting on the mainland about one mile across the water from Waadaah Island. There is a breakwater that stretches from the mainland to the island. Because

Waadaah Island Life-Saving Station was active during 1908-1910. The station was moved to Baaddah Point on the mainland following the tragic loss of two surfmen.
United States Coast Guard Academy

the breakwater is made up of rocks, it is very difficult to make the journey by walking this route. The best way to the former U.S. Life-Saving Service site is still by small boat. Winds can spring up quickly in the Strait of Juan de Fuca and suddenly cause a heavy chop, just as it did that night in 1908.

Waadaah Island at the time of the accident was a very isolated station. It remains out of the mainstream today. The location of the former station is within the Makaw Indian Reservation and permission to visit the island must be obtained from the Makaw Indian Nation tribal office in Neah Bay. Dense stands of Douglas fir, cedar and other flora common to a temperate rain forest environment characterize the reservation. To give an understanding of its remoteness, it is an hour and a half drive via a narrow, winding coastal road to Port Angeles, the only community of any size in the region. Occasionally the coast road will wash out and then residents will take an inland route that adds at least thirty or forty minutes driving time. One would expect, given this isolation, that the deaths of Surfmen Jacobsen and Sundstrom would soon be forgotten, especially since no trace of the old Waadaah Island Life-Saving Station remains. Instead, the opposite is the case.

Surfmen were attempting to reach this launchway at Waadaah Island Life-Saving Station when their dory capsized. Note Makaw Indian dugout canoe on launchway. Some surfmen here were Native Americans and Indian dugout canoes were a common sight at early Washington State Life-Saving stations. This launchway was later destroyed in a storm. United States Coast Guard Academy

Waadaah Island had the first standard 36-foot motor lifeboat in the Life-Saving Service, Conqueror, *shown here. It was probably the boat used the day the two surfmen were lost.* United States Coast Guard

In October 1995, eighty-seven years after the accident, with the permission of the Makaw Indian Nation, I visited the graves of Surfmen Jacobsen and Sundstrom on Waadaah Island. Chief Warrant Officer C. S. O'Neal, then commanding officer of U.S. Coast Guard Station Neah Bay, and his executive officer, Chief Boatswain's Mate Philip Spangler, provided me transportation in the station's 44-foot motor lifeboat. CWO O'Neal and Chief Spangler were my guides on the island.

Once on the dock of the island, one must climb about sixty or seventy feet above sea level to reach the graves. Most or all of the original timber on the island has been logged off and dense stands of alder, vines and other growth now abound. Passage is very difficult, not unlike trying to force your way through a jungle. Even while wearing the bright orange Coast Guard exposure suits from the trip on our motor lifeboat, it was almost impossible to see one another after a few feet into this dense growth.

What makes visits to the gravesite possible are the efforts of the Coast Guard Wives' Club, with some help from the station crew. The trail is hacked through the dense brush up the slope for perhaps two hundred yards or so. The amount of work to maintain this trail is great.

At the gravesite a high cyclone fence has been erected which surrounds a white picket fence. Neither is locked. Within the fence are Surfman Jacobsen's and Surfman Sundstrom's final resting places. There is a monument in the shape of a column that at some time in the past was broken off. On my visit, I noticed at one corner of the enclosure a small teddy bear. CWO O'Neal informed me that someone, other than from the U.S. Coast Guard, places toy animals at the site. The Wives' Club has taken upon themselves the care of the little cemetery as a special project. Through their efforts, at this remote location, a part of the U.S. Life-Saving Service is maintained and two of the many who died so that others might live are still remembered. This is, I think, a fitting tribute and link between lifesavers of the past, present and future.

THE RESCUES
•••--••• •••--••• •••--•••

Rescued From a Wave-Swept Rock
From the **San Francisco Call,** *March 15, 1899*

Edited by Ralph Shanks (Volume 2, Number 3)

FIVE short blasts and a long one from the lighthouse station on Point Bonita, California, created consternation in shipping circles yesterday morning (March 14, 1889). It was the distress signal, and the first time it echoed across the Golden Gate was when the mail company's steamer *City of New York* went ashore in a fog below the lighthouse (six years earlier).

When the (lighthouse distress) signal blew for the second time yesterday the wind was blowing 50 miles an hour from the northeast, the fog had shut down until it was impossible to see across the Golden Gate. Squall after squall struck the Point Bonita Lighthouse, and it was a nasty morning.

During the lull in the storm the lightkeeper fancied he heard a cry for help. He waited until the squall had passed. The cry came again, and again was drowned by the gale. The keeper made a tour of the reservation, but the fog was so thick that he could not see anything, nor could he locate the direction from which the cries came. It was then he sounded the distress signal.

Across the Golden Gate (at Land's End in San Francisco) John Hyslop was on the lookout for the Merchants' Exchange, while a short distance from him was the lookout for the Golden Gate Life-Saving Station. Hyslop was the first to make out the "distress signal," and he at once notified the exchange. It did not take long to let the tug companies know, and in a few moments the Shipowners' Company had the tugboats *Sea King* and the Spreckles Company *Relief* on the way to the scene. The *Sea King* had a good three-quarters of a mile start, but the *Relief* overhauled her at Fort Point and was easily the first to Point Bonita. Captain Clem Randall slowed down and made an examination of the shore line, but could see no trace of a disaster.

•••--•••

Point Bonita Life-Saving Service surfmen with breeches buoy struggled atop cliffs hundreds of feet high to rescues. Rodeo Lagoon, just north of Point Bonita, can be seen in the background. United States Coast Guard

Half a dozen crab nets were out, but there was no sign of the crab boats, and the captain remarked to his mate: "I wouldn't be a bit surprised if a few fishermen had been drowned."

From Point Bonita the *Sea King* and *Relief* went out through the north channel and up the Marin County coast as far as Bolinas. No sign of a wreck could be seen nor was any vessel in distress sighted, so both tugs returned to port.

In the meantime, the three San Francisco USLSS lifesaving stations had been notified and (keepers) Captain Hodgson of the Fort Point Station, Captain Varney of the Golden Gate station and Captain Smith of the South Side station soon had their boats in the water and under way. Smith and his crew had to go from four miles south of the Cliff House to Bakers Beach, as they could not launch their own boat, but even with that handicap they were not far behind the others. When they all got across the Golden Gate (to Point Bonita in the Marin Headlands) no trace of a disaster could be found. Captain Hodgson ran his boat in as close to the beach as possible and then jumped onshore, taking with him a gun and shot line. He clambered up the face of the cliff and joined the lighthouse keeper, who was waiting for him.

At that instant the cry for help came again. It seemed to come from the ocean side of the promontory and thither the men made their way. Another faint and despairing cry brought them to the cove where the new life-saving station is to be built (Point Bonita Life-Saving Station would not be built for several more years). The surfmen made their way around the cliff and heard the cry of help distinctly.

Clinging to a rock, over which the waves broke every few seconds, was a fisherman. His boat was not far away, bottom up, but the rock was the better refuge, and to it the fishermen clung.

Keeper Hodgson and the men from the lighthouse did not waste any time about getting the man off the rock. He was on the outermost end of a small reef and hard to get at, but with the aid of the Lyle gun and the shot line he was finally landed on the beach more dead than alive. The fishing boat, although capsized, was anchored, and after some dangerous work it also was secured, righted and anchored in a sheltered spot.

The crab fisherman's name is Antone Razeto. According to his story told in the lighthouse, he went out early to catch crabs. It was not blowing hard and he did very well. About 9 o'clock, it began to blow and he made up his mind to get back inside. An hour later, it was blowing a gale and the fisherman found he could not weather Point Bonita. He got into the little cove

Point Bonita Life-Saving Station stood atop the rugged cliffs rimming Bonita Cove at the north side of the entrance to San Francisco Bay. The station was built in September 1899 in response to numerous shipwrecks. The station no longer stands today, although the building which housed the beach cart survives. United States Coast Guard

and there came to anchor, but the big seas came rolling in and capsized the boat. He got on the bottom, but he washed off again and again. Then he managed to get on the rock and to it he clung, calling for help every time there was a lull in the wind, until his rescuers came. Had it not been for Captain Hodgson of the Fort Point Life-Saving Station, Razeto would have undoubtedly been drowned, as there are neither life lines nor boat at the lighthouse. To the lightkeeper belongs a good share of the credit, however.

On the way back from Bolinas the tug picked up the Life-Saving Service lifeboats and towed them to Fort Point. Razeto was too exhausted to be moved, so he was left at the lighthouse.

THE RESCUES

Braver Men Never Manned a Lifeboat

by Frederick Stonehouse (Volume 1, Number 2)

LOOKING back over a century of time, it is hard for us to fully realize the difficulties the old U.S. Life-Saving Service faced and the simple, matter-of-fact way they met and overcame them. The surfmen had a job to do and they would do their best, regardless of the danger. Sometimes, in spite of their skill and bravery, they were not successful. A case in point is the rescue of the crew of the schooner-barge *St. Clair* on October 1, 1888 on Michigan's Lake Huron shore.

About noon the steamer *Lowell* left Harbor Beach (then called Sand Beach Harbor), Michigan, on the west shore of Lake Huron bound for Bay City, about eight miles to the northwest around Pointe aux Barques. During this period in Great Lakes history steamers were replacing sail and it was common to convert old schooners, barks and brigantines into hybrid vessels known as "schooner-barges." The idea was to make obsolete sailing ships into barges that could be towed by a steamer. Generally conversion involved cutting down the top hamper and leaving only enough sail to keep from being blown ashore. A small crew of five to seven men (sometimes including a female cook) manned the schooner-barge. The crews faced great danger if the tow line parted and they faced a lee shore, since available sail had been reduced to a minimum during conversion. Anywhere between one and eight schooner-barges were towed in "strings" behind powerful steamers. Among others in the *Lowell* string that day were the schooner-barges *Lillie Mae* and *St. Clair*.

That October day the wind was blowing fresh from the north with a moderate sea and for a while presented no special problem. As the afternoon wore on the wind and sea increased. By late afternoon, conditions were bad

Harbor Beach Life-Saving Station. National Archives

enough that the steamer *Lowell* and her fleet could make no progress, so she swung around to return to the port of Harbor Beach. By the time they reached the harbor, the sea was too heavy to allow them to maneuver through the narrow gap between the two breakwaters. With no other choice, the steamer left her barges outside where they all came to a safe anchor. The *St. Clair* dropped both anchors about a half-mile leeward of the south breakwater and three quarters of a mile off the beach. The steamer sought shelter inside the harbor. Her captain later asked a tug to go out and bring his schooner-barges in, but the tug captain refused. The weather had become too rough.

Seeing the potential for trouble U.S. Life-Saving Service Keeper George W. Plough of the Harbor Beach (Sand Beach Harbor) Life-Saving Station launched his lifeboat and rowed out to the anchored vessels to see if help was needed. The first schooner-barge he checked was the *Lillie Mae*. She replied all was well. Moving on to the *St. Clair* and knowing that she was "old, rotten and unseaworthy," Keeper Plough urged her captain H.C. Jones, to leave her without delay.

The *St. Clair's* captain refused to abandon his ship. For a full hour Keeper Plough kept his lifeboat at the *St. Clair*, all the while trying to convince her master to leave her. In spite of the fact that the weather continued to worsen, the stubborn captain refused to go with the lifesavers. Torrents of sharp rain marched across the harbor and strong wind gusts buffeted the anchored fleet. Keeper Plough argued to Captain Jones that holding his crew aboard would make no difference when the storm struck, so they might as well get off while they could. The captain refused to heed the keeper's advice. One surfman later remembered the captain saying, "all he had was tied up in her and he would stick with her to the last."

Keeper Plough also asked if he could at least take the young woman who was the ship's cook to safety. She was Julia Greavreath of Sebawaing, a lakeshore community on Saginaw Bay. Seemingly taking her cue from the captain, she rejected leaving the ship. She would stick by her captain.

Since the captain steadfastly refused his pleas, Keeper Plough and his surfmen reluctantly returned to their lifesaving station. Having left hurriedly without donning their oilskins, the surfmen were chilled to the bone and the warmth of the station would be welcome. Returning to the station also gave the lifesavers the good tactical advantage of placing themselves windward of the fleet. Should their services be needed by one of the schooner-barges, they could reach her quickly. Before leaving Keeper Plough told Captain Jones that if he changed his mind, to burn a flare and they would return.

About 10 p.m., less than a half hour after returning tired and cold to the Harbor Beach Life-Saving Station, the lookout reported a torch burning on the *St. Clair*. It was the distress signal.

By now the wind had increased to full gale and a furious sea was running outside the piers. Knowing the extreme danger they were facing, the surfmen donned their oilskins and life preservers. Understanding too the great risk they were facing, the surfmen each gave the keeper's wife their valuables to hold before they left. It was the old motto again. "Regulations say we have to go out, but they don't say anything about coming back."

Realizing once they reached the *St. Clair* they would be unable to return to the station against the force of the sea, Keeper Plough decided he would have to run for the safety of the St. Clair River, sixty miles to the south and leeward of the schooner-barge. It would be a terrible trip, but it was his only option.

When the surfmen reached the rolling and pitching *St. Clair*, they had great difficulty working in alongside her. Finally, one of the men on the schooner-barge managed to throw a heaving line to the USLSS lifeboat and the sailors hauled the heavy lifeboat to the ship. Quickly the six sailors and Julia Greavreath jumped into the wildly tossing lifeboat. Once all were safely aboard, the lifesavers dropped the line and the lifeboat was swept out into the surging waters. Soon thereafter the *St. Clair* foundered.

What followed was an epic run over a wild and tumultuous lake. The surfmen started out under oars, but Keeper Plough soon had his crew set a reefed sail, steering with the tiller and two quarter oars. Time and again, the lifeboat was nearly smothered by a tremendous sea, breaking sharply and then rushing by on either side. For a time the Life-Saving Service cheated disaster. Finally, a monster wave broke over the stern, carrying away the tiller and nearly

Large boathouse at Harbor Beach Life-Saving Station. National Archives

causing the boat to broach. Recovering rapidly from this near catastrophe, Plough lowered the sail and ordered his men to continue under oars.

All night long, frigid waves periodically swept into the lifeboat, soaking surfmen and sailors alike before streaming out through the boat's drainage ports. One of the waves put out the lantern, preventing Keeper Plough from seeing the compass. When he called for matches, only one man had some that were still dry. The difficulty of relighting the lantern on such a terrible night can only be imagined: stinging spray, a pitching and rolling lifeboat, numbed fingers fumbling with an ever decreasing number of dry matches. But finally that lantern was lighted and the keeper brought the lifeboat back on course.

To have lost that feeble lantern glow would have been disastrous. Just holding the lantern and keeping it out of the water was a difficult job. Several men tried, but their hands got so numb they could not keep it up. Finally, Julia Greavreath took over the job and throughout the night kept the vital lantern burning. This courageous young woman was helping to keep them all on course and alive.

Throughout this wild night the Life-Saving Service's lifeboat again earned its well deserved reputation for strength and seaworthiness. The lifeboat could not be defeated. But the people on board were only human and they had limits. When the gray dawn finally broke, everyone on board was exhausted and suffering from hypothermia.

In a desperate attempt to keep the seas clear of the boat, Keeper Plough trailed an oil can. It did the trick, smoothing the seas enough to keep them out of the boat, at least as long as they were in deep water and the oil lasted. The oil was not used earlier because the can was stored under the deck and the keeper was afraid that if he tried to get it out in the darkness, an unseen boarding wave might strike and flood the open hatch.

With the dawn it was clear lifesavers and sailors, especially Captain Jones and Julia Greavreath, were exhausted and frozen to the bone. Going the full sixty miles to the St. Clair River at the southern extremity of Lake Huron was clearly out of the question.

Port Sanilac, however, was approximately halfway and when they arrived off the harbor at about 6 a.m., Keeper Plough decided they must try to land there. He would attempt to run the lifeboat into the lee of the 500-foot crib pier and onto the beach. Word of their epic run had preceded them and at least 200 people lined the shore to watch their life or death struggle. The crowd knew the storm warriors were out on the lake and coming their way.

In later years the Coast Guard built this Chatham-style lifeboat station to replace the earlier USLSS station at Harbor Beach. Michigan State Archives

The lifeboat soon arrived off Port Sanilac. Just as it passed the end of the pier a tremendous wave, piled higher by the shoaling bottom, caught the lifeboat and she broached. Another wave smashed into the lifeboat, rolling the boat completely over and throwing everyone into the boiling surf. The heavy lifeboat rolled three quarters of the way back toward upright, but before coming around entirely it struck bottom.

Eight of the sixteen people on board managed to get back into the lifeboat and eventually rode it to shore. Three others swam ashore, but five souls perished, including brave Julia Greavreath. Those that made it to the beach owed their lives to the efforts of bystanders, several of whom dashed into the surf to haul them to safety. Two of the surfmen were so far gone that they had to be carried off to bed for medical treatment.

As a result of their arduous training and the fact that they wore the regulation USLSS life preserver, Keeper Plough and all of his surfmen survived. In the terrible minutes after the lifeboat capsized, it was literally everyone for themselves. The already weakened sailors were easy victims of the hungry lake. Besides Julia Greavreath, three sailors and Captain Charles H. Jones were lost. If Captain Jones had heeded the Life-Saving Service's warnings off Harbor Beach everyone would have survived. Of Keeper Plough and his surfmen, the 1889 U.S. Life-Saving Service Annual Report wrote, "Braver men... never manned a lifeboat."

THE RESCUES
•• ----- ••   •• ----- ••   •• ----- ••

A Cape Cod Shipwreck and Rescue: The Case of the Horatio Hall *and the* H.F. Dimock

by William P. Quinn (Volume 1, Number 3)

EARLY on the morning of March 10, 1909, a volume of warm air moved silently in over Massachusetts' Cape Cod from the south. When this air encountered the cool ocean waters of the Labrador Current passing near the Cape, it condensed into fine particles of water and obscured vision around the peninsula. On that thick hazy morning, five miles east of the Cape Cod port of Chatham, two coastal steamers were wending their way - one north and the other south - through the Pollock Rip channel.

They collided.

The *Horatio Hall* of the Main Steamship Company was on her way from Portland to New York and the *H.F. Dimock* of the Metropolitan line was on her run from New York to Boston when the accident occurred. The *Horatio Hall* was a 3,167 gross-ton passenger steamer, built in 1898. She was 296 feet long with a 46-foot beam and driven by a 4,200 horsepower steam plant. The *H.F. Dimock* was a 2,625 gross-ton passenger steamer, built in 1884. She was 271 feet long with a 41-foot beam and powered by a 2,000 horsepower steam plant.

The bow of the *Dimock* penetrated twenty feet into the port side, amidships, of the *Horatio Hall* and that vessel began to sink immediately Captain Thompson of the *Dimock* sensed the danger to the other vessel and held his vessel on her forward motion and thus moved the *Hall* to shallower waters where any possible salvage could be accomplished much more easily than if the ship were down in deep water. This action also enabled the passengers and crew of the *Hall* to climb over the wreckage and go aboard the *Dimock*. The *Horatio Hall* soon sank on the shoals to the point where her

•• ----- ••

hurricane deck remained above water. Captain Jewell and four crewmen stayed aboard the sunken vessel to protect the ship from salvagers. The *Dimock* remained at the scene for three hours and the resumed her trip north to Boston. But the ship was slowly sinking because of the damage done to her bow in the collision. The forward bulkheads were holding but Captain Thompson decided to run her ashore to save her from going to the bottom.

While sounding her distress signals, the vessel came to the beach about two o'clock in the afternoon a half-mile below Cape Cod's Orleans Life-Saving Station. Capt. James Charles, the keeper, alerted his men and they hauled out the lifeboat. They launched the boat into the surf and rowed towards the noise of the distress signals. As the fog lifted, the lifesavers arrived at the grounded vessel and went on board. Capt. Charles and his men then brought a number of passengers ashore and telephoned the keepers of the nearby Old Harbor and Nauset stations for assistance. It required thirteen trips with the lifeboat through choppy seas to land sixty-seven passengers and crewmen from the *Horatio Hall* on the beach in Orleans. The survivors all walked to the Orleans Life-Saving Station that afternoon where hot coffee, doughnuts and biscuits were served to the appreciative group of survivors.

Later in the afternoon, the people were taken to Orleans center where the local residents opened up their homes and took all the survivors in for the night. This type of succor would be unheard of today but those were different times and more considerate people. The *Yarmouth Register* newspaper reported in the March 13, 1909 issue that: "Capt. James Charles and the surfmen had their hands full making frequent trips to the ill-fated vessel and doing what they could in the way of rendering assistance to her crew and passengers. The latter were taken care of admirably by the town. Previous to their departure for their various points of destination on Thursday morning, they were provided with comfortable lodging, supper and breakfast. Thus, once more did the lifesaving station ably justify its maintenance on this shore and the townspeople unmistakably demonstrated their ability to meet the requirements of the hour at a time of emergency."

The next day, all of the survivors left in the morning after the Orleans selectmen had obtained passes for them on the train. Our story does not end there. The Orleans lifesavers were kept quite busy using their lifeboat as water transportation for the Underwriter's agents and salvage teams busy trying to save the *H.F. Dimock*. Capt. Jewell remained on the *Horatio Hall* until the next day and then abandoned her to the elements. The Chatham fishermen did not let this opportunity slip away, however, and within a matter

The H.F. Dimock *ashore at Orleans, Massachusetts, after the collision with the* Horatio Hall, *March 1909.* Tales of Cape Cod, Inc., Barnstable, Massachusetts

of hours they were on board the vessel stripping everything that wasn't nailed down and in some cases, even that did not deter them. The insurance agents reported that there was nothing left to take. The unknown salvagers had even taken up the rugs from the floors. They had left nothing. A question of recovery of property was raised but when the crew that had remained after the accident left the vessel, she was fair game for one and all. There are quite a few souvenirs in and around Chatham to this day from the *Horatio Hall*. Her quarterboard can be seen at the Cranberry House on Main Street.

The next few days were filled with activity on the beach in front of the lifesaving station. Crowds of people rode down the back roads on the beach in their horse drawn buggies to view the wrecked vessel. At one point there were one hundred people reported sitting on the dunes behind the wreck watching the salvagers at work repairing the huge holes in the bow of the ship in order to refloat her. On the 11th, four tugboats arrived on the scene and began the wrecking operations. Three days later, they pulled the *Dimock* off the beach and she was towed to Boston for repairs. The *Horatio Hall* lay on the shoals off Chatham for a short time until it was determined that she was a menace to navigation in that area and had to be blown up. Most of the hull, however, is still there and is a mecca for SCUBA divers in the summer. Apparently the Chatham fishermen didn't get everything off the steamer as the divers still find salvageable pieces on the wreck.

••·--·••

Orleans Life-Saving Station played a central role in the H.F. Dimock *and* Horatio Hall *rescues. Grateful survivors presented Orleans surfmen with a silver pitcher to show their appreciation for being brought safely ashore.* Shanks Collection

This accident was very similar to an earlier one by the *H.F. Dimock* at approximately the same location. Early in the morning on July 23, 1892, the palatial yacht *Alva* was anchored in Pollock Rip Slue in dense fog when the *Dimock*, running on her route to New York, crashed into the port side, aft, of the 285-foot *Alva* and caused her to sink.

The yacht was owned by William K. Vanderbilt and had been built at a cost of $500,000. Mr. Vanderbilt and his guests were all asleep at the time of the accident and were rudely awakened by stewards who rushed them on deck in their pajamas and robes to be loaded into the ship's boat which had been readied just after the collision. The entire ship's company was taken aboard the *Dimock*, which suffered extensive damage to her bow plates but was still able to remain afloat. The *Dimock* was at the scene until just after noon and then continued on her trip to Boston were Mr. Vanderbilt, after landing, was immediately on the telegraph to arrange for a new yacht. One would almost think that the *Dimock* should have been declared a menace to navigation around Pollock Rip Slue.

THE RESCUES
••• --•••   ••• --•••   ••• --•••
Only Once On Lake Huron
by Frederick Stonehouse (Volume 1, Number 4)

ON May 30, 1889, Lake Huron was churned by a vicious northeast gale. Up and down the broad lake, vessels ran into trouble and the lifesaving stations were forced into action.

At 3 p.m. veteran Keeper George Plough and his Harbor Beach (Sand Beach Harbor) crew used their surfboat to rescue the watchman from the schooner *Eugene*. Lumber laden, she was anchored behind the breakwater when powerful wind blasts snapped the anchor chains, sending her rolling for the beach. The lifesavers pulled the watchman off just before the vessel hit. The rest of the schooner's crew was safe ashore, apparently on a "saloon sail" when the accident occurred.

Keeper Plough had no sooner brought his crew back to the station when they were called out again, going to the aid of yet another vessel. The station lookout had spotted the steamer *C.M. Chamberlain* slowly working her way through cresting seas and driving rain toward the harbor. Since the lookout could plainly see she was riding low in the water, there was obviously something seriously wrong. Just as she slipped behind the breakwater, the steamer lost all power when the boiler fires finally flooded out. The action of working in the rising seas had sprung a couple of the *Chamberlain's* planks and several feet of water were sloshing about in her hold.

When they rowed out to her, the lifesavers learned the *Chamberlain* had earlier dropped her tow, the schooner-barge *Victor* of Hamilton, Ontario and that the *Victor* was likely headed for the beach somewhere off to the south. The pair were bound from Midland, Ontario, to Buffalo when the nor'easter overtook them.

••• --•••

After arriving at the city dock, Plough sent his number one surfman with the rest of the crew back to the station for the surfboat and beach apparatus. All crews were organized by the "numbers," with the number 1 being the most experienced and number 7 the least. Keeper Plough then went on ahead alone to reconnoiter. Using his big marine glass, he soon spotted the wreck about three and one half miles to the south and in the breakers 150 yards or so offshore.

A crowd of townspeople had gathered on the beach waiting in eager anticipation for the lifesavers. A roaring bonfire provided an eerie glow to the scene and also signaled the shipwrecked victims that help was on the way.

At about 9 p.m. his crew arrived, having arranged for horses to haul both the beach cart and surfboat. The wind continued to blow viciously from the northeast and rain drove hard on the lifesavers. Although decked out in full storm gear, it wasn't a fit night out for man nor beast and would only get worse. Looking hard at the crashing waves Plough decided to use the breeches buoy. Using the breeches buoy at night with only the feeble yellow glow of a lantern for light wouldn't be easy, but the surfmen had drilled both night and day for this eventuality.

Turning around, he took the leather haversack from the number 1 surfman then ordered the cart placed between the spot he selected for the sand anchor and the surf. His well-trained crew knew the drill well and only a minimum of instructions were needed to set them into motion. When the keeper gave the order, the surfmen responded. Number 4 threw the canvas breeches buoy off the cart, while numbers 5, 6 and 7 unloaded shovels, the pick and wood sand anchor, then set to work burying it. Numbers 2 and 3 removed the faking (shotline) box. Plough and number 1 picked up the heavy Lyle gun off the wagon bed and positioned it four or so yards to the windward of the cart and roughly aimed at the wreck. Surfmen numbers 2 and 3 inverted the shotline box and placed it on line with the gun and a yard to windward. After lifting the pin section clear, they angled the box with the carefully faked line toward the wreck.

After estimating the distance and wind force, Plough determined the charge and slid a powder cartridge into the gun. Meanwhile number 1 selected a shot, wiped it as clean and dry as was possible under the storm conditions and held it as number 2 wet a fathom of line then bent it on the shank with three half hitches. Wetting the line was necessary to prevent it from burning from the fiery muzzle blast. In the driving rain, it didn't seem to be necessary but the rules were the rules. Standing well to the side, number

Harbor Beach Life-Saving Station and crew. Captain Ted Richardson

1 slid the projectile carefully down the bore until it rested on the powder charge. He also assured there was no slack between the gun and shotline box. If there was any the terrific acceleration of the shot would break the light line.

Numbers 1 and 2 positioned themselves on their knees to either side of the gun. Plough reached down and pricked the power cartridge leaving the priming wire in the vent hole. He then kneeled to the rear of the gun. After carefully considering the wind force and direction, Plough ordered the men to move the gun left or right until he was satisfied with the aim. He then stepped forward and adjusted the elevation with the combination level. He quickly removed the priming wire from the vent and inserted the primer, bending a 90-degree loop at right angles to the tube. Hooking his firing lanyard into the loop, he carefully wove the lanyard through the rear handles of the gun carriage to assure the pull wouldn't disturb the elevation. He then stepped back and to the windward side and waited for just the right moment, when the gale moderated slightly he yelled, "ready". A moment later, he pulled firmly on the lanyard and Lyle's little gun barked in response sending the projectile sailing off just to the north of the vessel. But just as Plough planned, the wind billowed the shotline neatly across the wreck.

The men on the *Victor* were busy too. When they recovered the shotline they rapidly started to haul it in hand over hand. Once the tail block reached the *Victor*, Captain Silversides yelled to his men to make it fast to the foremast. On shore Keeper Plough had his portion of the breeches buoy rigged and his surfmen ready. With Plough's sharp commands of "man the whip" and "haul off" the surfmen went to the tee whip and pulled the breeches buoy out to the wreck.

Once the first sailor climbed into the swinging buoy, Keeper Plough shouted at his crew to, "man the weather whip, haul off" and the first victim headed for shore. Once ashore, Plough and his number 7 surfman helped the sailor out of the awkward device. There were both women and men still on board the ship and the breeches buoy was immediately pulled out again.

The next man rescued was also a sailor. The third person brought ashore by breeches buoy was Minnie Silversides, the captain's twelve-year-old daughter. The fourth was the schooner's cook, a woman who weighed more than 200 pounds. The three men still aboard the wrecked ship had great trouble trying to squeeze her bulk into the breeches buoy. The cook was so heavy the surfmen later complained to little Minnie that they thought they "were pulling the vessel ashore." True to tradition, the last man ashore was Captain Silversides. Soon after, the *Victor* was destroyed by the pounding lake.

Throughout the rescue, the schooner was alive, with each crashing wave she slowly bounced closer to the shore. Because of the vessel's movement, after each breeches buoy cycle, the lifesavers had to stop and carefully tighten the hawser again, but not too tight for fear of pulling the mast over.

The breeches buoy was an integral part of the lifesaver's arsenal of weapons against death. The crews drilled with it until they could successfully execute the intricate evolution night or day, fair weather or foul, in the warm breezes of a cloudless July afternoon or with frozen fingers in a numbing spring gale. As identified by his number, each surfman had a specific job. Once the keeper judged that his crew knew their numbered responsibility, he switched them around, so each also learned the other's job. Throughout the history of the service, crew proficiency in the drill proved critical to achieving success under the most arduous conditions.

Although his recollection could certainly be in error, veteran Keeper Henry D. Ferris claimed in an 1898 interview that the *Victor* rescue was the only time the breeches buoy was ever used by a Lake Huron crew. Ferris was keeper of the Harbor Beach Life-saving Station from February 1911 until it became Coast Guard in 1915. Considering the operational lives of the nine Lake Huron Life-Saving Stations, a notional seven month season of 30 weeks with a drill every week, meant a minimum of 35,280 breeches buoy drill iterations for a pay off of only one actual rescue! Certainly for young Miss Minnie Silversides, her dad and the men and woman of his crew, it was all worth the effort. Lake Huron may have seen such an unusually small number of breeches buoy rescues because it has comparatively shallow water along its shores. Vessels would have stranded so far offshore they were beyond the range of a Lyle gun and rescue had to be by surfboat and lifeboat instead.

THE RESCUES
A Sunday Evening in the Pacific Northwest
by Dennis L. Noble (Volume 4, Number 1)

AT 2:30 in the afternoon of Sunday, November 14, 1998, U.S. Coast Guard Station Cape Disappointment, Washington, received a call from the fishing vessel *Miss Renee*. *Miss Renee*, a gill-netter, had the net on a large reel located on the bow. The skipper of *Miss Renee* stated his engine had failed and he needed assistance. The U.S. Coast Guard station at Cape Disappointment guards the treacherous Columbia River Bar on the Washington-Oregon border.

Miss Renee's skipper seemed confused as to his location. Two of Cape Disappointment's motor lifeboats, the 52-foot motor lifeboat *Triumph*, and a 47-footer, happened to be training in the area. The two motor lifeboats located *Miss Renee* and *Triumph* took the boat in tow to Ilwaco, Washington.

The mouth of the Columbia River is one of the most treacherous areas for mariners in the world. Near the last bit of man-made structures that try to control the river – north and south jetties – the river is approximately one-and-a-half-miles wide. It is also near this location that a unique feature of the West Coast of the United States enters the picture. The depth of the water begins to shallow and forms what sailors call a bar. When the ocean waves go from deep to shallow in a very short distance they "feel bottom" very rapidly. In other words, the seas begin to drag along the bottom and this causes steep waves. The steeper the waves, the more chances for them to break, and breaking waves are the most powerful seas a mariner must face. This is bad enough, but in the Columbia River area the sailor is faced with even more dangers provided by nature. In winter, many of the low pressure systems that enter the United States come ashore some place in the state of Washington, causing high onshore winds and rain. Added to this witch's brew is the tidal action of the ocean. During the winter months strong onshore winds begin pushing ocean waves against the bar, while the powerful outflowing from the river meets the forces of the incoming tide. At the Columbia River bar it is not unusual for a mariner to face steep breaking waves of twenty or more feet. The area is known as the "Graveyard of the Pacific."

The U.S. Coast Guard station sits on a northerly channel off the Columbia River that enters Baker Bay and the town of Ilwaco, Washington. Motor lifeboats from the station must travel approximately 1-1/4 miles along the channel in a southerly direction to reach the Columbia River. From this location, known as "the gates," a coxswain will turn the boat in a southwesterly direction and travel for about 7 miles to the entrance buoy of the river. If the motor lifeboat must go upriver, the coxswain will turn in a south-easterly course. The largest city in the immediate area, Astoria, Oregon, lies some 17 miles away in this direction. The river is very broad in this area. The main shipping channel of the Columbia River both upriver and downriver to the mouth is well marked with aids to navigation, such as buoys, both lighted and unlit, and daymarkers. Overlooking the mouth of the river is the Cape Disappointment lighthouse located high on a cliff. Next to the lighthouse is a U.S. Coast Guard lookout tower.

As the evening of Sunday, November 14 approached, the weather, as usual, began to deteriorate near the mouth of the Columbia River. At 4:18 p.m., the communications watchstander at the Cape Disappointment station again received a radio call from *Miss Renee*. The skipper informed Seaman (SN) Aaron E. McCollum that he wanted to go across the Columbia River to Astoria, Oregon. The skipper wondered if the weather conditions were good enough" and whether it "was advisable or not."

McCollum contacted the station's Officer-of-the-Day (OOD), Boatswain's Mate First Class (BM1) Stephen Schuch, and informed him of *Miss Renee's* request.

BM1 Schuch had McCollum radio the fishing vessel the current weather conditions only and inform the skipper that the safe navigation of his vessel was his responsibility. The U.S. Coast Guard is not allowed to tell commercial fishermen if the weather is safe to operate their vessels; they can only repeat the weather.

McCollum transmitted: "The condition of the river at this time is about a three to four foot wind chop, the winds are about 40 knots. It will soon be getting dark. The decision to go to Astoria is entirely up to you." The skipper of *Miss Renee* acknowledged the call.

Almost an hour later, SN McCollum received a call from the communications watchstander at U.S. Coast Guard Group, Astoria, Oregon. McCollum learned that the wife of the skipper of *Miss Renee* was on the telephone. The wife was patched through to McCollum. The Cape Disappointment watchstander learned that the skipper of *Miss Renee* had called his wife on a cell telephone and told her they were in a sand spit near the gates. McCollum told the wife he would call the skipper on the radio and see if he was okay.

The skipper responded he was fine. McCollum asked the skipper to give the station a call when they reached Astoria. No sooner had the skipper of *Miss Renee* told McCollum that everything was fine, then he informed the watchstander he was unsure of his location. He said his engines had cut off. Steve Schuch recommended that *Miss Renee* anchor. At this time, Schuch learned the fishing vessel had no navigational equipment aboard.

BM1 Schuch made the logical conclusion that the fishing vessel was at some location upriver in a line from the gates to Astoria. Recall, to reach Astoria, from Ilwaco, the skipper of *Miss Renee* would travel southward along a marked channel out of Baker Bay, passing by the U.S. Coast Guard station on the way, until reaching the Columbia River and then turn southeasterly to make the 17 mile transit across the river to Astoria. The forces of nature also entered heavily into Schuch's decision-making. The winds, from 40 to 50 knots, were screaming from the south, thus a boat should be pushed onto the Washington side of the river and away from the dangerous bar. Furthermore, with the tide flooding, the current would be into the river, again pushing *Miss Renee* away from the dangerous bar.

Schuch ordered the ready motor lifeboat, *CG 47207*, and ready boat crew to get underway. BM3 David M. Chapman II, a 47-foot motor lifeboat coxswain, would be in charge of *CG 47207*.

The U.S. Coast Guard does a very poor job of informing the public, and especially the news media, of the various levels of expertise of the coxswains operating the boats at small boat rescue stations. A person who is a coxswain is able to take a boat out in most weather and is in complete charge of the boat. The coxswain must be checked out in each type of boat at a station. A coxswain in a 44-foot motor lifeboat, for example, must become checked out in the 47-foot motor lifeboat before being placed in charge of that type of motor lifeboat. In the Thirteenth Coast Guard District (Washington and

Oregon) a coxswain is not expected, and indeed is expressly forbidden, to take a boat out into extreme conditions, such as in breaking surf. Only a surfman, the highest level of boatmanship in the U.S. Coast Guard, is permitted to operate a boat in these conditions. The service's regulations state very clearly that a surfman will be aboard any boat in breaking surf. Like a coxswain, a surfman must be checked out in each type of boat at a unit. At the time of the *Miss Renee* incident, BM1 Steve Schuch was both the OOD and the duty surfman. Schuch could operate the 52-foot motor lifeboat, one that is much slower than the 47-footer. The service's failure to inform people of these qualifications and limitations would greatly affect those who worked the *Miss Renee* incident on this gale-whipped November night.

As Chapman and his crew of *CG 47207* got underway, BM2 David W. Jussila, off duty, returned to the Cape Disappointment station for the evening meal. Jussila heard the SAR announcement and "went up to the comms room to offer my assistance."

Jussila's giving up his off duty time is an example of how, when a search and rescue (SAR) case happens at a small boat rescue station, it galvanizes the unit and makes everyone want to do something. It is difficult to explain this to a person who has never served aboard a station. I have even felt it at units that were in the midst of major cases, so much so that I, after being retired for more than 20 years from the U.S. Coast Guard, offered to help, BM2 Jussila's offer to help would prove to be extremely useful.

While Chapman and the *CG 47207* sped out to the Columbia River, BM1 Schuch tried by radio to determine *Miss Renee's* location. The captain of *Miss Renee* told Schuch he could see a flashing red light. On the tapes of the radio transmissions one can hear Schuch telling the fisherman, "If you could look at that light and time it one thousand one, one thousand two, and give me the amount of seconds between each flash."

Back came: "Twelve seconds approximately."

Schuch then felt the skipper was looking at the Cape Disappointment lighthouse.

BM1 Schuch transmitted: "Look at the red light and then at your compass and read in degrees the direction the lighthouse is pointing from your boat."

Shortly after this, the *CG 47207* asked *Miss Renee* for a long count on the radio to get a fix with directional finding equipment aboard the motor lifeboat.

With the bearing, and radio direction finder, BM1 Schuch plotted the actual position of *Miss Renee*. Somehow the skipper of the fishing vessel had headed southwest instead of southeast. The captain of *Miss Renee* had miscalculated

Fifty-two foot motor lifeboat Triumph *in action in heavy surf on the Columbia River bar on the Washington-Oregon coast. Larry Kellis, Coast Guard Auxiliary*

his course by at least 90 degrees. If the U.S. Coast Guard had not told him to come to anchor, there is the very good chance that he would have run into the south jetty. As it was, *Miss Renee* now sat at anchor very near the Columbia River Bar, in the area of Clatsop Spit known among U.S. Coast Guardsmen at Cape Disappointment as "death row," because of its high surf.

Chapman, meanwhile, headed toward the location. Once Chapman informed Schuch he was in the Clatsop area, Steve asked if there was surf. If surf existed, Chapman would have to pull out of the area, as he was not authorized to operate in those conditions.

Dave responded, "No breaks (breaking waves). It's pretty rough."

Schuch asked for depth.

"19 feet."

Schuch again asked if there was any surf where the fishing vessel was anchored, or if Chapman would have to transit through surf to get to him.

"We're in Clatsop right now. No breaks."

A short period of static-filled silence.

The radio crackled and Dave said, "I don't know if we are going to be able to get in close enough to get a hold of him."

Schuch asked Chapman why he cannot get close enough.

Silence.

"We just took a break about 16-foot. We're transiting out of Clatsop now. Request launch second boat now."

Later, David Chapman would say "My crewman yelled, 'Break!' I turned the boat into the break, which was estimated to be about 16 feet. Shortly thereafter a second break came." Chapman and his crew took a total of three breaking waves.

Once BM3 Chapman started out of Clatsop, he radioed *Miss Renee*, "Have you seen any breaks in your position?"

"No. Have some big rollers rolling in here."

When listening to the taped radio conversations with *Miss Renee* there is never a sound of worry in the voice of the captain of the fishing vessel. Normally, even the saltiest fisherman's voice will rise slightly when in imminent danger. This can lead to the conclusion the captain had no idea of his location and no notion of the danger.

BM1 Steve Schuch now had BM2 Jussila take over the OOD watch. After assigning Jussila a series of tasks, Steve took the motor lifeboat *Triumph* out into the gale-swept night. Following orders, Jussila called BM1 Jeffery Kihlmire, another surfman, at home and told him to return to the station. BM1 Kihlmire was the only surfman checked out on the 47-foot motor lifeboat. Jussila called U.S. Coast Guard Group Astoria and requested they launch a helicopter.

Miss Renee's captain over the radio: "Did that other boat turn around and go back?"

SN McCollum informed the skipper that *Triumph* was en route to them.

"That's the one that towed us in earlier. Great. Thanks."

Cape Disappointment station asked *Miss Renee* if they had flares aboard and they replied that they did. Shortly thereafter, the skipper of the fishing vessel asked: "We was wonderin' when you thought their ETA (estimated time of arrival) might be?" For the first time there is a hint of worry in the voice. Another question from *Miss Renee* asking the position of *CG 47207*.

BM1 Steve Schuch, aboard *Triumph*, radioed BM3 Chapman about the conditions he encountered approaching *Miss Renee*.

Chapman replied, "On our inbound run we took a series of three 16-foot breaks. He (*Miss Renee*) was about 300 yards from us, straight on the knuckle (a geographic location used by Cape Disappointment coxswains to locate an area near the south jetty entrance to the Columbia River)."

A little after this exchange, Chapman tried to raise *Miss Renee*. There is silence. After a pause, "Fishing vessel *Miss Renee*, this is U.S. Coast Guard *47207*."

BM1 Jeffery Kihlmire was off duty at home preparing to go to a birthday party when the telephone rang at about 6:00 p.m. BM2 Jussila "told me a boat was disabled and in the surf in Clatsop Spit. I needed to come in and get the *47207* to backup the duty surfman, who was already going out on the *Triumph*."

Kihlmire, a 13-year veteran, has 11 years of experience at small boat rescue stations on the East Coast, West Coast, Great Lakes, and again back to the West Coast. He made surfman in 1996.

Later, Jeff Kihlmire would say "At the point when I left the house, all I knew was there was a boat in Clatsop and they had lost communications. I assumed it was capsized."

BM1 Schuch later said, "I advised my crew we were going into the surf in Clatsop Spit to look for a vessel with three people aboard. Visibility was reduced to about 50 yards as we headed out. Once in the channel the spotlight burned out. We used radar to navigate the rest of the way through the channel."

Once in the Columbia River the visibility improved to one half of three quarters of a mile. BM1 Schuch navigated *Triumph* to buoy number 12, near the reported location of *Miss Renee*. He waited there until *CG 47207* could return with BM1 Kihlmire aboard. *CG 47207* would travel approximately 2.25 miles from the station to rendezvous with *Triumph*.

"I met the *207* at the dock and did a quick debrief with the coxswain and sent him up to the comms room," said BM1 Jeff Kihlmire. "I took his crew back out." Kihlmire also took FS2 James W. Maggs, one of the station's cooks. Jim wanted to help, but was not boatcrew qualified. Kihlmire knew that if he had survived aboard the 47-foot motor lifeboat, regulations state there must be a crewman in the survivor's compartment with the rescued people. By having Jim Maggs with any survivors he could have his boat crew on deck. Maggs, like all people attached to the Cape Disappointment crew, is first aid qualified.

"It couldn't have been more than five or six minutes later I rendezvoused with the 52-footer (*Triumph*) between buoy 10 and 12, just outside of the surf line in Clatsop. We decided to spread out and start lateraling in. We staggered ourselves, with the 52 leading. I was a little more seaward. About the time we got half-way across the helo (*CG 6003*, a HH-60 Jayhawk from Astoria) overflew us. They spotted the overturned boat and spotlighted it. I was in the faster boat and able to get there quicker than the 52."

"When the pilots called in the boat, I don't think they could see the guy sitting on the stern. When we got close enough, one of my crewmen could see someone wavin' on the stern."

Boatswain's Mates Steven Schuch, left, and David Chapman II, right, discuss the location of the rescue. Dennis L. Noble

BM1 Kihlmire started piloting the motor lifeboat toward the overturned hull. The wind, seas, and aspect of the overturned boat did not allow for a typical rescue of a person in the water.

"I couldn't get upwind from it – the wind was out of the south and the seas were coming from the west," said Jeff Kihlmire. "The overturned boat was anchored and sitting cockeyed to the wind. With the bow being anchored and the heavy surf had even more action on it. The boat would pop up and the wind would catch the stern, which was sticking out of the water, and try to blow it down wind. The surf would knock it back the other way. It was a stationary object, not moving with the current much, pushed back and forth by the wind and current."

Normally, the coxswain would put the bow of the motor lifeboat into the surf and come in upwind. Then the coxswain times it so when moving up to the person in the water, the survivor is on the leeward side of the boat. The wind has more effect on the boat than the person in the water, so the boat will be blown to the person. What Jeff Kihlmire faced was an overturned boat in the surf, which meant he could not come upwind, as he would be blown down on top of the boat and the person clinging to the hull. In addition, Kihlmire did not know whether the gill net from *Miss Renee* was loose below the boat. If so, he ran the danger of having his screws fouled and ending up on the beach.

In spite of this, BM1 Kihlmire tried to rescue the person using the approved standard method. In winds of 50 knots, low visibility, and rain coming at him horizontally BM1 Kihlmire maneuvered *CG 47207* toward the overturned *Miss Renee*. As he worked closer, Kihlmire fought the bow of the motor lifeboat as it moved toward the person clinging to the hull. Kihlmire broke off. In the heavy gale and driving rain, Jeff again steered the motor lifeboat toward the survivor. The slightest mistake would cause the motor lifeboat to come crashing down on the victim. The motor lifeboat's bow again drifted toward the hull. Kihlmire broke off the approach.

What to do?

"I know the 47 will take a pretty good swell on the stern," Jeff later said. "We're talking 8 to 10 foot. I knew if I planed into the wind, it would put me in the right position no matter which way the stern of the *Miss Renee* swung. It would give my crew more time and allow me to sit there longer.

"I lateralled into the surf zone and then I drove straight at the stern of the boat where the guy was and I power pivoted. You split the throttle and turn the wheel. In this case, I turned down-swell and pivoted the boat around.

"The first approach we made in this manner, we slid close to them. We got a line to him. He could hold onto it. The surf went by and engulfed both of us. I pulled away to make sure I didn't come down on the boat.

"We tried it again. This time I got closer. The first throw into 50 knots of wind got to him, but blew away. So, the crew pulled it in real quick between the breaks. I kicked the boat a little closer. The crew just threw the rat's nest of the line. It wasn't pretty. It just fell all around him. He had no choice but to grab it. I was six to eight feet from the boat. They pulled him to the boat. My two crewmen were on the starboard side trying to get the guy aboard.

"My engineer was up on the coxswain flat with me. He yelled, 'Break comin'!'"

One aspect of working in high seas at night that gets the adrenaline pumping and the imagination working overtime is not being able to see what is out there. You know it has to be big. Surfmen have said no matter how much noise the weather is making, you can hear the big ones coming. Out of the darkness you hear what sounds like a train approaching.

"You could hear it coming," said Jeff. "It was too dark to see it. I had the boat lit up like a Christmas tree to see the guy. You could see the reflection from the top of the white water.

"I yelled down to the crew, 'Hold onto him!'

"They had him about half way into the boat. Break hit us. Splashed over the stern. It completely covered up the crew in white water.

"I had the boat bladed (cocked) away, so the port side of the stern took the impact to protect the crew. The boat leaned to starboard and just scooped him up into the boat. Once the break went by, I looked down and all three were in the well deck. So I beat feet out of there."

The survivor was taken into the cabin by a crewman and Jim Maggs. The crewman came up and informed Kihlmire that the man said one person had drifted away. He had a strobe light blinking. Then the chilling news that a boy was trapped beneath the hull.

BM1 Kihlmire immediately radioed the Cape Disappointment station about the situation. Almost as soon as the radio message went out, the helicopter spotted the strobe. The helo's rescue swimmer went into the water to help hoist the man.

Kihlmire's motor lifeboat now was getting pushed into shallow water. Jeff recalled the depth at around ten feet. The boat crew started to discuss how they could get the person out from under the hull.

"My crew volunteered to go into the water and try swimming under the hull." (I can later recall Jeff looking at me and saying, "Dr. Noble, do you realize how many Coasties have been killed doing that?")

Kihlmire continued, "Someone who was a qualified free swimmer would have had a difficult time. The bucking and pitching of *Miss Renee*. Not knowing if the bow net reel had come loose and if the net was floating underneath the boat. Our standard operating procedure says a swimmer must have a lifejacket and be tethered to the boat. It was hard enough to swim in the surf. The risk was too high. I ruled that option out real quick."

The crew discussed other options, but, as Jeff pointed out, "just dealing with a capsized, anchored boat in calm water in a current is a tricky maneuver with a small boat," but with something almost 30 feet long in the weather conditions we faced made it almost impossible.

"I kept reaching into my bag of tricks and nothing would work. A series of large breaks came in and the *Miss Renee* was gone," Kihlmire recalled.

BM1 Kihlmire then called the station and told them they had lost sight of *Miss Renee*. Other U.S. Coast Guard boats soon arrived and Kihlmire was ordered back to the station to drop off the survivor. Shortly afterwards, Kihlmire returned to the search. Eventually, the one person plucked from the stern of *Miss Renee* was the only one who survived.

Anytime a small boat station cannot save someone, the crew feels despondent. Even though BM1 Jeffery Kihlmire performed an amazing feat of boatmanship to rescue the one survivor, most on the station felt down.

The news media now enters the picture.

Television news broadcasts demanded to know why an "unqualified" person was on the 47-foot motor lifeboat. Why did the motor lifeboat turn back? Perhaps if the U.S. Coast Guard had a good system of informing the media of the weather in which their coxswains can operate, the media would have realized BM3 David Chapman made the correct decision and the innuendoes would not have been bandied about.

Both BM3 David Chapman and BM1 Jeffery Kihlmire made agonizing, but correct, decisions on the night of November 14, 1998.[1] Recall a captain in U.S. Coast Guard headquarters telling me BM3 David Chapman "had the balls to make a decision I am not sure many captains in headquarters could make." I would add that both of these young men made tough decisions that most U.S. Coast Guard admirals in headquarters have never had to make and then were made to feel guilty about their work.

Every once in a while in life, people who do good things are rewarded. For his outstanding boatmanship in this rescue, BM1 Jeffery Kihlmire received the Meritorious Service Medal, with operational device. For their work in helping to bring the survivor aboard the motor lifeboat, crewman SN Arron Birdsong and BM3 David Leighton received the Coast Guard Commendation Medal, with operational device. The boat engineer, MK1 Matthew Calvert, and volunteer FS3 James W. Maggs both received the Coast Guard Achievement Medal, with operational device. Most importantly, on Tuesday, September 28, 1999, the Association for Rescue at Sea, an independent civilian organization, voted to award BM1 Jeffery Kihlmire their Gold Medal for Lifesaving, thus certifying the work of BM1 Jeffery Kihlmire and the U.S. Coast Guard station, Cape Disappointment, Washington, on November 14, 1998.

THE RESCUES
How Many People Will a Lifeboat Hold?
by Ralph Shanks (Volume 1, Number 4)

HAVING spent the past two decades writing maritime history books, my work has allowed me to become friends with many a veteran surfman. One of those I remember especially well was Garner Churchill. During the 1930s Chief Churchill had been the commanding officer of the Humboldt Bay Coast Guard Lifeboat Station near Eureka, California. He ran 36-foot wooden motor lifeboats out of both Humboldt and San Francisco Bays and saved at least 300 lives from shipwrecks. Mr. Churchill was perhaps the greatest lifesaver in Pacific Coast history. What Joshua James was to the Atlantic Coast, Garner Churchill was to the Pacific Coast.

The motto of these brave Coast Guard lifeboatmen was "You have to go out, but you don't have to come in." This meant that regulations required that the surfmen go out to the rescue no matter what the sea conditions were, but there was no guarantee they would ever return.

One of Garner Churchill's finest rescues involved the rescue in 1931 of the steam schooner *Cleone* off Cape Mendocino. When Churchill and his men reached the sinking ship they encountered huge waves and a sea full of 30-foot long bridge timbers that had been the *Cleone's* deck load. The bridge timbers were 30-feet long and 14-inches square and they were heavy on one end. Having been torn off the sinking ship by the sea, the bridge timbers floated vertically in the storm tossed waves. They would sink far below the surface and then suddenly rise up on a big swell and fly into the air and then fall over. Garner Churchill told me that "If even one came up under (the Coast Guard motor lifeboat), I'd have been a goner."

Garner Churchill of Humboldt Bay Lifeboat Station near Eureka, California, receiving the Congressional silver medal circa 1940. Chief Churchill was offered the gold lifesaving medal and his motor lifeboat crew was offered the silver life-saving medal. Churchill refused to accept any medal higher than the one offered to his Coast Guard crew and thus accepted a silver medal instead of the gold one the Coast Guard wanted to award him. Garner Churchill photo in Shanks Collection

But Garner Churchill piloted his lifeboat in among the flying bridge timbers. Maneuvering skillfully he took everyone from the *Cleone* safely on board his rescue boat. Once away from the wreckage, Churchill faced a new problem. His lifeboat now had so many people in it that it was so low in the water it was barely afloat. Yet eventually, Garner Churchill managed to reach a safe harbor and brought everyone ashore alive.

After he told me this story, I asked Garner how many people his motor lifeboat would hold. He looked up and smiled. "I never found out," he replied.

I sat there in silence thinking of the magnitude of what this great lifesaver had just said. He was saying that no matter how great the risk there was always room for one more person in his lifeboat.

THE RESCUES
"Get the 36 Boat Going, NOW!"
by Frederick Stonehouse (Volume 2, Number 4)

SOMETIMES simple things turn terribly tragic. A perfect plan just crumbles and the result is disastrous. An example happened at Oswego, Lake Ontario, New York on December 4, 1942.

Oswego old-timers remember it as the worst gale in thirty years. Not since the infamous 1913 freshwater hurricane tore through Lake Ontario was Oswego pummeled by a storm of such intense ferocity. Powerful winds of 65 mph blew steady, tearing out trees and snapping down electric power and telephone lines. Huge waves marched into the harbor, pushing rocks weighing several tons around like a child's wooden blocks. One five-ton boulder was rolled over the breakwater! Snow drifted heavily across the landscape further adding to the feeling of desolation.

Far out in the Oswego West Pierhead Light the lighthouse keeper, Boatswain's Mate First Class Karl A. Jackson, waited with increasing impatience. The frenzy of the storm had marooned him in the isolated tower for the last three days and he was ready to leave his lonely prison. Five times he blew signals with the foghorn asking for relief. "Where were they?" Rations were getting short and he was just plain hungry!

The breakwater lighthouse, built in 1930, sits on top of a square concrete foundation. It is about 10 feet from the water to the top of the landing deck. A steel ladder set in the concrete provided access from the water. The structure perches at the west end of the west breakwater, about a half-mile offshore.

Just past 10:00 a.m., the 38-foot wooden picket boat left the Oswego Coast Guard Lifeboat Station at East Cove and headed for the light. The small boat drove on through the cresting gray waves, shouldering them aside as it continued to work its way slowly to the light. Aboard were two relief keepers, Bert E. Egelston and Carl Sprague, and eight other Coast Guardsmen. The six extra men were needed to help fend off the boat when it lay alongside the concrete foundation of the light to transfer the keepers. Although the boat would be under the lee of the breakwater and sheltered from the worst of the storm, additional help was needed. Lt. (j.g.) Alston J. Wilson, 54, the commanding officer of the station, captain of the port and a 35-year Coast Guard veteran, was in command of the boat.

By the time the boat left the station the storm had moderated, with the wind down to 30 mph and the waves somewhat diminished, but it was still very rough. Although the conditions were bad, Wilson believed the transfer could be safely made.

He was right. The transfer was made successfully. Wilson carefully brought the picket boat up to the ladder, the extra men fended it off, and both men scampered up the steel rungs to safety. Timing his move gingerly, Jackson dropped down the ladder and jumped into the tossing boat without injury. To this point it was a job well done.

The boat backed away from the concrete foundation of the light easily, but when the gasoline engine was shifted into forward, it inexplicably quit. The boat immediately started drifting fast, west to east, right across the harbor mouth and began a violent motion, caused by the enormous waves and powerful current from the Oswego River. Twice, the engineer, Machinist's Mate First Class Fred Ruff was able to start the stalled engine in the small engine room. Each time the balky engine quickly coughed to a stop.

Lt. Wilson then ordered the 125-pound anchor dropped to check the boat's drift. Second Class Seaman Irving Ginsburg and Second Class Bos'n's Mate Eugene C. Sisson crawled out on the iced-up and violently pitching bow and released it.

The anchor immediately dug deep into the soft bottom of the harbor. The bow of the picket boat swung into the wind and the progress toward disaster was checked. Now there was time to either get the engine going or for a rescue boat to come out from the station and tow them back to the dock. Then the inch and a half manila anchor line snapped. In the powerful wind and waves it had held for a bare ninety seconds.

At the outer end of the east breakwater was a small beacon known at east light. It was protected by a rock barrier. Now began a fight between wind and current. If the wind won, the boat would hit the east breakwater at a point

Oswego Lighthouse and breakwater rocks. Scene of the 1942 Oswego Coast Guard Lifeboat Station disaster. United States Coast Guard

where there was some protection afforded by the west breakwater since it was partially under its lee. Although the boat would be lost, the men would likely be safe. If the current proved the stronger, the boat would probably end up in calmer water, allowing time for either repair or rescue. The combination of the two forces, however, kept the boat trapped in a deadly course for the sharp edged rocks surrounding east light.

The testimony of Chief Bos'n's Mate John Mixon, the second in command of the station, and Machinist's Mate First Class Fred L. Ruff, the only survivors, can recreate the last moments of the boat.

Lt. Wilson was in the small pilothouse with Ginsburg, Sisson and Mixon. The first two men soon went on deck, apparently uncomfortable in the small, closed-in cabin. Before Wilson followed them on deck, he turned the wheel over to Mixon. Adrift, or not, the wheel must be manned. Jackson, First Class Seaman Leslie J. Holdsworth, and Second Class Machinist's Mate Ralph J. Sprau were on deck in the aft cockpit. Ruff was in the engine room still desperately trying to get the engine working. Mixon remembered Wilson as utterly calm, giving orders as if he were back in the office. Disaster may be imminent, but he kept his wits clear!

The boat was being driven rapidly eastward, parallel to the breakwater. The bow was pointing toward the shore. They would be all right, if they only would clear the end of the rocks.

A large wave surged under the boat and sped it towards the murderous rocks. Realizing what was happening, Wilson yelled, "Look out, she's hitting!"

The boat crashed on the port side with tremendous force, the impact shattering her planking and rolling her over, dumping the men on deck into the frigid water. The backwash swung it out to sea with the bow facing out into the lake. As the boat righted itself, another wave again smashed it into the rocks, tearing a hole ten-foot long and three-foot wide into the starboard side. The overturned boat then drifted off into the lake.

Mixon was trapped inside the pilothouse and only escaped by smashing out a window and diving through it into the water. When he finally surfaced, he was being carried along by the current but was able to grasp a jagged rock at the end of the breakwater. With a strength born only of desperation, he somehow was able to climb the slippery rocks of the ten-foot high breakwater to safety. He didn't remember how he did it.

Ruff recalled when the boat first rolled, the engine room flooded with three feet of water let in through a ventilator hatch. After it righted and hit again, he scrambled out through the hatch to the deck. Finding himself ten feet from the end of the light, he quickly considered the situation then jumped for it. After a short swim he also reached safety at the breakwater.

From his rocky perch on the ice covered breakwater, Mixon looked for his shipmates. Other than Ruff, he saw five or six men left struggling in the rough water. Sisson was about 60 feet away, desperately trying to swim to the breakwater. Both were caught in the current and being rapidly carried out into the lake.

All the men were struggling to reach the rocks. Wilson and Ginsburg were swimming in the lee of the east breakwater. Jackson was holding onto the broken anchor line that was still fast to the picket boat. The boat itself was barely awash and drifting 300-400 feet to the east.

Wilson's oilskins had trapped an air pocket, which was helping the officer to stay afloat. When a big wave pushed him closer to the breakwater, Mixon, although exhausted and shaking uncontrollably from the cold, scrambled down the rocks with the intention of diving in to help him. When Wilson saw Mixon's intent, he calmly told him, "Don't try it. Save your own life, John." Wilson then stopped struggling. He had issued his last command.

Ginsburg continued his fight to reach the rocks. For a while he swam overhand. Then he tried sidestroke and later backstroke. Unable to beat the powerful current, he finally just sank forever beneath the cold waves.

Jackson soon loosened his death grip on the anchor line, dropped off and sank, too. Some observers on shore thought he might have managed to climb on the bow, only later to slip off into the lake. In the blowing scud and snow they could not be certain just what they saw.

Mixon and Ruff slowly began to work their way from the outer end of the 2,100-foot breakwater toward shore. The breakwater did not extend all the way to the beach. There was a gap of 250 feet between it and land. For a while they crawled painfully on hands and knees to keep from being swept into the lake. Countless times they slipped on the icy rocks and fell. Each time they got back up and fought onward toward the shore.

When they saw the picket boat was in trouble, the men at the station sounded the alarm and desperately worked to get a rescue boat underway. Second Class Bos'n's Mate Robert Burnet, left in charge of the station, bellowed, "Get the 36 boat going, now!" The big 36-foot motor lifeboat was on its cradle in the boathouse and had already been laid-up for the winter. But their shipmates were in danger and with unheard of speed, it was oiled, fueled, serviced and run down the rails into the water. It took a bare 18 minutes to get going at full throttle, bashing its way through the seas to the rescue. Burnet was at the helm. Six other Coast Guardsmen stood ready for action in the cockpit.

Afraid to try to lay the motor lifeboat directly against the rocks of the breakwater to rescue Mixon and Ruff, Burnet sent two men, Coxswains

The classic 36-foot wooden Coast Guard motor lifeboat. United States Coast Guard

Sanford Gregory and John F. Black, over in a small skiff trailing a line back to the lifeboat. By this time Mixon and Ruff had made it about 1,600 feet down the breakwater. The hope was to get both men into the skiff, then haul it to the big boat with the line. However in the fury of the gale, the skiff smashed against the rocks, stranding both rescuers and victims and losing the line in the process.

Deciding that Ruff and Mixon and his two men were in less immediate danger than those farther out, Burnet pulled away and headed out for the awash picket boat. When they found Wilson's body still floating, he asked for a volunteer to try to recover it. Seaman Second Class Andrew W. Cisternino volunteered, tied a rope to his waist and dove into the furious 40-degree water.

He reached the body and grabbed it tightly but as he was being hauled back to the boat, the cold numbed his arms and the body slipped away in the waves. Only with the greatest difficulty was the boat crew, numbed with cold and balancing precariously on the icy deck, able to drag Cisternino back aboard. Wrapped in blankets he was hustled below. When the boat eventually reached shore, he was immediately hospitalized for exposure.

To those on shore, the rescue effort was especially dramatic. The motor lifeboat repeatedly disappeared in the trough between the huge seas, giving the impression that it too had sunk. Each time it reappeared to continue on with its work.

Anxious family members waited at the Coast Guard dock for the lifeboat to return. Some hoped their men on the ill-fated picket boat had somehow been saved from an icy death. Others prayed for the safe return of the rescue crew.

With no other choice open to him, Burnet decided he had to risk the boat to rescue the four men on the breakwater. He knew that a mistake on his part could not only wreck the boat but put his crew into the same circumstance that the picket boat men ended up in. Using every ounce of skill and experience, Burnet brought the big boat right up to the rocks and neatly picked off the stranded men. It was a masterful piece of seamanship! The four bedraggled men were taken below to join Cisternino, and Burnet headed for the dock.

Ruff, Mixon and Gregory were immediately hospitalized. In a classic case of understatement concerning Burnet's work in rescuing them, Mixon said, "Bob did a fine job."

The broken, battered picket boat soon washed ashore and Coast Guardsmen waded out waist deep into the surf to search for the bodies of their shipmates. None were found in the battered boat. For several days, following the disaster,

Coast Guardsmen and soldiers from nearby Fort Ontario patrolled the windswept beaches looking for bodies. Their efforts were fruitless.

History has a way of repeating itself. An old-timer remembered that during the 1913 gale lighthouse keeper Dan Sullivan was marooned at the west light for a full week. Part of the time he, too, was without food. After signaling his wife of his predicament, she told a friend who managed to fight his way out through the tumultuous lake with provisions. In 1913, it was tragedy averted. In 1942, it was death at Oswego Lighthouse.

The tragedy and heroism of that terrible day was ignored for over half a century. Happening when it did, in the midst of World War II, other events captured the public imagination. On December 4, 1996, 54 years to the day, the Coast Guard and the City of Oswego formally memorialized the event. Survivors of the accident, family members and representatives of the city boarded the station's 44-foot motor lifeboat and motored to the vicinity of the disaster and placed a memorial wreath in the icy waters of Lake Ontario. The solemn ceremony occurred at 10:25 a.m., exactly the time of the 1942 accident. The City of Oswego also plans to erect more permanent memorials, one near the lighthouse and the other in Veterans Park.

One of the participants was David Ginsburg, the father of Irving Ginsburg, killed in the wreck. Now 98 years old, he vowed never to return to Oswego until some kind of memorial was established. It took a long time, but finally the brave men received the recognition so richly deserved.

THE RESCUES

•••--••• •••--••• •••--•••

A Brush With Coast Guard History:
At Sea On February 19, 1952

by Frederick G. "Bud" Cooney (Volume 5, Number 1)

THAT February night in 1952 was bitterly cold and exceptionally black in the city of Portland, Maine. All supplies needed for this patrol had been stored away. All loose gear below decks and topside had been stowed, secured, or lashed down, ready for sea. The captain was informed that the ship was ready to get underway.

The main engines of the 311-foot Casco class cutter *Cook Inlet* (WAVP 384) were fired up, giving new life to the ship. The gangway, our only bridge to shore, was hauled aboard and lashed secure. Light snow began whipping about in a gusty wind. All this activity was new to me, and I felt excitement mixed with a little tinge of fear of what was coming on my first weather patrol since graduating from Coast Guard boot camp at Cape May, New Jersey. A couple of seamen from the cutter *Acushnet* (WAT 167), tied up aft of us, were stationed at the bollards to handle the mooring lines. They soon became aware that the number 2 line and the bow line were frozen solid to the pier, and would have to be cut when we were letting go. Fire axes were provided to accomplish this task.

Word passed over the loudspeaker system to "Set the special sea detail, man mooring stations, prepare to get underway." There was great movement of personnel about the decks for a couple of minutes, and then relative calmness set in as the word came to "Take in number 2 line, take in the bow line." Finally all lines were let go or chopped free and we were underway. The ship glided slowly away from the pier. There were hand waves farewell from the cluster of friends and relatives huddled in the cold dim light on the pier. Smiles were not part of this picture. It wasn't a happy time for anyone, for it would be about five weeks before we would tie up here in Portland once again. This was not a departure for a pleasure cruise. Danger lurked about in the vast bleak cold North Atlantic, and heartache and longing waited for those left on land.

We were all convinced that the job we were heading out for was real, was important, was risky and was our duty as Coast Guardsmen. We were trained to save lives and property at sea if called upon, carry out our designated responsibilities as the United States seagoing law enforcement agency, and to collect important weather data to provide ships at sea and trans-oceanic aircraft vital meteorological information to guide them on their journeys.

Another deckforce seaman and I were ordered to get below to the aft hawser locker to stow mooring lines as they were fed to us from the main deck. Every evolution aboard this ship was a new learning experience for me and there was always a boatswain's mate nearby to instruct on how things were to be done and when to do them. Soon after I entered the hawser compartment I heard the loudspeaker blurt "Secure the special sea detail and set the sea watch." By this time I was crawling about on top of three-inch hawsers stowing them in a neat coil. The manila rope was wet, cold and rather stinky. The compartment was damp and close.

I was both chilled and sweaty as I became aware of the rhythmic vibrations of the screws as they lifted up and settled back into the swells, a new sensation. From what I had heard from others, I was well on my way to becoming seasick, another first for me as I never had been on the open ocean before. Yes, this was it, a dizzy head and a jumbled stomach. Would it pass? Would I get used to it? How would I tend to my tasks? Here we were only starting out, and I had weeks to go before I would set foot on land again. I had trouble trying to fathom the concept of what days and weeks of this perpetual motion really would be like. Only time would tell.

The duty messenger (watchstander) came down from the bridge with a weather report hanging on his clipboard, informing all concerned that a full gale was catching up to us as we were headed up to Argentia, Newfoundland, to top off our tanks with diesel fuel for the long and rough trip into the Atlantic. I recall thinking, "This weather is enough for me now, what the hell is it like in a gale?" The watch list posted in the port passageway told me that, in addition to a multitude of other tasks, I would be standing the 8-12 lookout/helm watch starting at 0800 the next morning.

The first night underway was emotionally and physically strange and exhausting. The motion of the ship set my new world rocking like nothing I had felt in my eighteen years on terra firma. Making my way along passageways, up ladders, and through hatches without sea legs left me feeling foolishly out of control and hindered my ability to take charge of my God-given motive skills. My world was unstable.

The weather topside was not pleasant, although the crisp salt air was rather refreshing compared to the eclectic ambient smells below deck. The night was cold and windy with only the white froth of the wave motions visible as I gazed out from the deck rail, no land in sight. I had learned in the previous hours since we left the safety of port that I would make my foul weather jacket

Frederick G. Cooney began life in the Coast Guard as a seaman aboard USCGC Cook Inlet *in the North Atlantic in 1952. Bud Cooney*

and a metal bucket a part of my personal shipboard gear, the jacket to throw on if I could make it topside to purge myself and ease the sick feeling, or otherwise use the bucket as a catch basin. These items became my underway security blanket for the next few weeks. I soon learned, without calculation, which was the leeward (lu-ard) and which was the windward (win-ard) side of the ship. This information was crucial to the routine of spilling my guts over the side.

Word came over the loudspeaker from the bridge, "2200, lights out in all berthing compartments, silence about the deck, the smoking lamp is out." I settled back into my rack. The red glow of the battle lantern (night light) mounted low on the bulkhead next to my rack gave a sober atmosphere to the whole scene around the berthing compartment. It felt good to lie flat on my back with my head cradled in my pillow to keep it from rolling to and fro. I listened to the strange sounds of the steel hull creaking, the rattle of the metal lockers, and I could sense the up-and-down floating motion of my mattress. I guessed it would be safe to fall asleep, as no one else about me showed any indication of concern. Oh well! The next day we would pull into Argentia just long enough to top off and head back out to Ocean Station Charlie 1500 miles out in the middle of the Atlantic. Would I last 'til then? When would I get my sea legs?

The shrill of the bos'n's pipe came over the ship's PA system, "Reveille – up all hands." I rolled out onto the moving deck as the berthing compartment lights came on. I felt woozy and somewhat apprehensive about going to the mess deck to face morning chow. I prompted myself to carry on and carry out my assigned tasks of being a seaman – without breakfast.

It was February 19, 1952. I listened to a radioman telling about the SOS that they had copied and the bits and pieces of the big "job" we had missed. The word came from headquarters via radio that we were too far out and must proceed on course to our ocean station destination.

The nor'easter we were pounding against for the last day or so had taken its toll on two large T-2 type tankers as they labored in sixty knot winds and sixty foot seas, only forty miles apart, east of Cape Cod. The events that were taking place outside our reach involved an armada of Coast Guard ships, Coast Guard aircraft from Salem, Massachusetts, and Quonset Point, Rhode Island, as well as smaller 36-foot Coast Guard motor lifeboats (MLBs) from Cape Cod and Nantucket, Massachusetts, and numerous trained Coast Guard personnel at shore stations. These were the rescue units that pulled together the humanitarian efforts from which many heroic acts and courageous deeds emerged during those dramatic days, the 18th and 19th of February, 1952.

Out on the cold, snowy, wild Atlantic where the wind reached seventy knots, only one battered T-2 tanker, the *Fort Mercer*, was able to send her SOS, as she was breaking in half in mountainous seas on the 18th of February. The Coast Guard heard the *Fort Mercer's* distress call and focused all attention on saving those desperate souls on board. The Coast Guard cutters, open lifeboats and aircraft fought howling icy winds and pounded wild seas to reach the scene of the broken tanker.

The second T-2 tanker, the *Pendleton*, had also split in two and drifted helplessly in the turbulent seas, undetected. The tragedy happened so fast that she was left with only radio receiver capabilities. Thirty-three souls held on, clinging to the stern section and listening on a radio receiver as the rescue cutters headed at best speed toward the *Fort Mercer*, miles away.

A vigilant chief electronics technician, his eyes glued to the small radar at the Chatham Lifeboat Station, saw what appeared to be two sections of another ship. As the stern section drifted close by the Pollock Rip Lightship, the Coast Guard crew could detect the name *Pendleton* on the floating storm-tossed hulk that held survivors on deck. This now confirmed that not one, but two ships had split in half in the storm.

Calculating that the stern sections of the *Pendleton* might come ashore near the Chatham Lifeboat Station at North Shore, Cape Cod, the officer-in-charge at the station had his crew prepare the beach apparatus to execute a rescue from the beach. It soon became evident that the stern section would clear the shore and drift past. The beach rescue operations were belayed.

It was time to send a lifeboat out into the raging seas to rescue the *Pendleton* men. Attempts to send a Coast Guard amphibious DUKW and a motor surfboat out from the Chatham station proved to be too much as the raging winter winds and the turbulent seas breaking over the sandbar forced them back to the dock.

Lieutenant Commander Frederick G. "Bud" Cooney, USCGR, visited the CG 36500 in 1992, forty years after it was used in the rescue of the crew of the Pendleton *off Chatham, Massachusetts. Bud Cooney*

THEY HAD TO GO OUT...

The task, to reach the half-frozen and desperate survivors on the stern of the *Pendleton*, fell to Boatswain's Mate First Class Bernard C. Webber and his young crew of the 36-foot MLB. Webber was coxswain, Engineer Second Class Andrew J. Fitzgerald was boat engineer, and Seaman Richard P. Livesey along with Seaman Irving W. Maske made up the heroic crew of the *CG 36500*. As they left the Fish Pier at Chatham on that horrifying night they all knew their humanitarian and Coast Guard duty instructed that they had to go out, and may not return.

Their first, almost impossible challenge was to get out beyond the treacherous sandbar. Despite ten-foot crunching rollers and howling wind-driven snow, almost no visibility, and the fact that the turbulent seas and gale winds tore the canvas canopy shattered their windshield, ripped the compass off, and carried most of their lifesaving gear overboard, Webber and his heroic crew hung on, stood fast, and brought the rugged motor lifeboat across the bar and into deeper waters to continue their mile or so roller coaster ride out to the *Pendleton*. Now, with no compass, the only navigational directions needed for the *CG 36500* crew to reach the wreck had to come from the vigilant radar operator at Chatham Station via two-way radio.

The thirty-three cold, desperate men huddled on the stern section of the *Pendleton* spotted the dim spotlight on *CG 36500* cutting through the darkness coming toward them in one instant, and disappearing in the black trough in the next instant. Bos'n Webber and his crew heard the distraught shouts through the howling winds and seas, coming from the helpless souls on the tossing hulk of the *Pendleton*. The MLB crew mustered all their boat handling skills to maneuver their small lifeboat to a dangerous position under the tossing stern. A rope ladder was hung over the ship's rail and the survivors, one by one, made their way down and clambered aboard the battered 36-foot rescue craft. For forty-five terrifying minutes the crew of the *Pendleton* climbed to safety. Three half-frozen men missed their drop from the Jacob's ladder to the bobbing boat, though two of them were hauled aboard the *36500*, while the third was crushed and lost, as the seas bashed the MLB against the steel hull of the wreck.

The wet shivering survivors took refuge in the cramped forward cabin and aft cockpit. Now it was time for the overcrowded small lifeboat with her wet, cold and tired crew of four and thirty-two survivors to make its way back to safety. With no compass, coxswain Webber turned the motor lifeboat for home. This maneuver probably would have ended in disaster if it were not for the expert help from the radar operator at the Chatham station. Chief

Electronics Technician W. H. Woodman tracked the *CG 36500* blip on his small search scope and directed Bos'n Webber by two-way radio with left and right turns that guided them on a safe course back to the Fish Pier at Chatham.

Thanks to God and the Coast Guard rescue team, all thirty-six people on board the seaworthy 36-footer made it back, battered, cold, wet, and, most importantly alive. The four young Coast Guardsmen of the *CG 36500* received the highest award possible for their heroic deed, the coveted Gold Lifesaving Medal.

This account of the *CG 36500* is only one segment of the spectacular rescues made during the storm off Cape Cod on February 18-19, 1952. Incidents of courage, devotion to duty, and outstanding seamanship were evident during the rescue of 70 seamen from the two broken tankers, the *Fort Mercer* and *Pendleton*. The entire mission during that winter nor-easter involved large cutters, small motor lifeboats, and Coast Guard aircraft backed by teams of shoreside men and women who demonstrated that we were all, including myself and my crewmates aboard the *Cook Inlet*, "Semper Paratus," always ready.

THE RESCUES
New Year's Eve, 1953
by Dennis L. Noble (Volume 5, Number 1)

MASTER Chief Boatswain's Mate Thomas D. "Tom" McAdams, U.S. Coast Guard (Retired) is a legend among those who serve at the motor lifeboat stations along the Pacific coast. If one uses national publicity as a guide, then Tom McAdams is the most famous enlisted man in the U.S. Coast Guard since 1915. During his time in service, he appeared in *Life*, *National Geographic*, *True* and other national media. CBS's Charles Kuralt featured the Master Chief on network television. He even showed up on an episode of the television series *Lassie*.

Tom developed two distinctive trademarks: a modified pilot's helmet which he wore while on a motor lifeboat to protect his head and keep his "ears warm," before the U.S. Coast Guard had a policy for wearing helmets aboard motor lifeboats, and an ever-present cigar. The cigar became a part of the McAdams mythology, something Tom did little to scotch. Charles Kuralt learned of it while riding a motor lifeboat with the Master Chief. The standard refrain heard up and down the coast was "As long as the cigar is lit, you can relax. But when it begins to get soggy, that's when you have to pay attention. If he takes the cigar out, turns it around and sticks the lit end in his mouth, then you know you're going to get wet. If you ever see him spit it out, then you'd better take a deep breath because you're going to have to hold it a long time (as the boat rolls over)."

He was highly decorated for his work at motor lifeboat stations. Some of his major awards included the Legion of Merit, one of only a few Coast Guard enlisted personnel to receive this award; the Coast Guard Medal, the highest award for valor that a person at a station can receive in peace time;

the Gold Life Saving Medal; the Coast Guard Commendation Medal; and the Coast Guard Achievement Medal. His civilian awards include an Oregon Governor's Award; the City of Newport (Oregon) Valor Award; and the Newport Chamber of Commerce Award for Civil Achievement. Tom retired from the U.S. Coast Guard in 1977.

Master Chief Tom McAdams is also a master at telling stories. In a long interview with Tom, I learned just how good he is. I thought the readers of *Wreck & Rescue Journal* would be interested in one of the Master Chief's stories. I selected one dealing with the old wooden 36-foot motor lifeboat. I edited it very lightly keeping the sense of Tom telling the story. The Master

Tom McAdams may be the most widely recognized Coast Guardsman of this century. United States Coast Guard

Chief uses a nice technique while spinning his tale, and brings his voice up to full volume at appropriate places. This is reflected in the account.

The incident he describes took place on New Year's Eve, 1953, when a fishing vessel called in from the Yaquina Bay Bar off Newport, Oregon with engine problems. McAdams, then a Boatswain's Mate First Class, went out from the Yaquina Bay station with an engineer as his crewman. Another 36-foot motor lifeboat also went to provide back-up. By the time Tom and his crewman got the fishing vessel in tow and started in across the bar, it was dark.

"The skipper, (Warrant Officer) Lawrence, got on the radio and said, 'Do not, not attempt to come in. It's now ebbing. It's dark. Stay out overnight. I'm getting the *Bonham* (a 125-foot cutter) to come relieve you of the tow.' The *Bonham* is in Bravo 6, which means they have six hours to get underway. Then they have to come eighty-six miles from Coos Bay. They're not going to be here until 10-11 o'clock in the morning. I'm going to spend a long, cold-assed night out here.

"I had my little air force helmet on to cover my ears. Bare pants. Foul weather jacket and the big old-fashioned life jacket on.

"I throttle down to save on fuel. My engineer was seasick. Pukin'. I'm going to be on the wheel sixteen-eighteen hours. Son of a bitch! It is going to be like getting a bucket of salt water thrown in my face every fifteen minutes for sixteen hours. That's the name of the game. So I throttled down and set myself to do it.

"In about fifteen minutes the engine went 'errrr.' Died. I knew what it was. The way the engine died. I knew what it was. The line was in the screw (propeller). How'd I get a line in the screw when I was towing ahead?

"I got on the radio. I started pounding on the radio and, all of a sudden, it works!

"The fisherman's calling me. He'd fixed his oil line, started his engine up and probably put it in gear. That put slack in the hawser. Even though I'm going ahead, I'm going so slow I took one of these big fifteen or twenty foot swells and I went up a swell an' came back on the swell. Probably sat right on the hawser.

"I got on the radio and said we got the line in the screw. We're disabled. The guy said, "I'll tow you to sea.'

"'No, you can't do that. You'll tow me from the shaft. You'll tear out my shaft and then I'll sink. We got the other lifeboat. Throw off. I still don't know how long you'll run. I'm still responsible for you. You go to sea. You get to safety. Let me go.'

"So he did it. He threw off the line.

"Now I've 700-800 feet of line trailing behind me and all around the screw. I call the other lifeboat. He comes out to get me.

"The lifeboats have a low profile. You had two little sidelights and a bow light that you pulled up. We always left it down, because if you pulled it up, it made a big glare and you couldn't see. So I had my bow light down and my little stern light, it's only six feet off the water. You can't see it, hell, for more than three or four hundred yards. The other lifeboat couldn't find us.

"The wind is blowing and gusting up to fifty miles an hour. I scudded right across the channel and I'm at the north reef. I'm going to hit the north beach somewhere between there and Yaquina Head.

"I got to get the anchor out. So I run up forward and open up the ready box. There's two anchors. A hundred pounder on the bulkhead and a fifty-five pounder. I can't handle the hundred pounder by myself, so I grab the fifty-five pounder. Broke it out. Did all the good things to get it ready. You got up to 300 feet of line. Throw on a good bowline and throw it overboard. Make the line fast. We drifted slowly and then the anchor slowly set.

"I told the other lifeboat where were at and he finally came to get us. I said, okay I'll cut this anchor line. Can't cut it because something could happen and I would need this anchor. So, I pulled. I had to actually pull the lifeboat ahead with the wind blowing. I pulled that lifeboat ahead all by myself. I pulled 360 feet of line in with fifty-five pounds of deadweight. I got the whole thing up. I'm exhausted.

"When the other boat comes, they've got the heaving line. I then had to pull in the towing hawser and make it fast. They then took me in tow. We went out where the rest of the fishing boats were.

"Then the fishing boats went in.

"Big steep swells. No breaks.

"So the lifeboat starts towing me in. Gets right off the can buoy. Then in comes a breaker. Hits us in the ass. We surf down it. Boat capsizes. The breaker hit the other boat in the stern. Runs him ahead. Broke the towing line like it was a piece of string.

"I'm up in the bow. Jump into the bow cockpit.

"I say, "Oh, shit!' I'm heading for the north jetty now.

"There used to be a can buoy outside the north jetty. I'm pulling in this tow line 'cause it broke somewhere along the line. Pullin' it in.

"All of a sudden I see the other lifeboat comin'. He's comin' back. CRASH! We hit the can buoy. Took a chunk off the gunnel. Bounced off. Now we're headin' for the reef.

"He's just about to us and he tosses us the line. He comes in and he's only got one man with him, too. I grab his towing line, but I don't have my snapped line bent (tied) to his yet. You make a Becket bend (knot used to join two lines of unequal sizes). I grabbed that line and went around once, then twice – I made a double Becket – dropped it down and made it tight. You got once chance. Oh, Christ, will that knot hold?

"BOOM! He jerks us around and it held.

"We called the Depoe Bay boat and came on up. He's got twelve miles to run. He got lost. It's gettin' close to midnight. He finally gets there. Now they say the bar's really good. Big swell, no breaks. So we transfer tows.

"I take this line off and throw it overboard and the other guy pulls up. So when he pulls over he's got an end comin' over fifty feet of line. Anyway, the other guy throws me the old heaving stick.

"Jesus! The old heaving stick is a piece of bamboo with three pounds of lead. Across the bow it came. I had to pull his line over, because he threw me a heaving line. All this time my engineer is holding a searchlight. That's his job, holdin' the searchlight. He's seasick. So I pulled that hawser up and make it fast to the tow bitts.

"I say, 'Go!' He starts in.

"My engineer took off his lifejacket. Puke all over it.

"'Put it on. They're going to tow us in. Put it on.'

"He couldn't. The old lifejackets had leg straps that went down over the groin and around. So I tightened them up with big square knots.

"I said, 'I don't like this.'

"So, I went up forward and grabbed the sea anchor. Big old canvas thing. I stream it (put it over the side). Just a straight sea anchor and now he's got me in tow.

"He starts across the bar. Now I got a sea anchor. I'm not going to ride a breaker and crash into him and capsize.

"Along comes a big series. Get to the top and the old sea anchor opens up and grabs me by the stern and jerks me back. This breaker breaks right off our bow. It breaks and hits the other lifeboat in the stern. Broke his tow line. He's inside the jetties. He thinks he's towing along like crazy, thinks he still has us in tow.

"Well, by this time the wind has switched and came out of the west. The current had started to flood and we're goin' across the south reef. We're headin' right for it.

"Oh, God! So, I get on the radio and start beatin' on the radio (to get it to work). Made three calls: 'This is NWEO! The tow line has broke! We're goin' on the south reef!' Said the same thing three times. Dropped the radio. Ran up the catwalk. Crawled across the forecastle on my hands and knees and jumped into that hole with my lifejacket on. Engineer's holdin' the searchlight….

"Then, I hear 'wooossh.' Look over my head. There she is. There's the old widow maker. We start to run with it. As we are running with it – 'wooossh' – ten ton lifeboat starts to surf a little bit. That… drogue opened on up and drug me back and made me go broadside as it drug me back.

"Lookin' twenty feet in the air at this thing comin' down. Black. Blowin' like hell. Middle of the night. You're soaking wet. You're getting tossed up and down. Rolled all around.

"Looked up in the air and yelled: 'HAAANNG ON!'

"I hung on.

"I ducked down in the cockpit. You stand up in the cockpit, you're up to your waist. In the bottom of the cockpit are two scuppers, one at each side so the water can run out. I ducked down until my head was probably just below the deck surface of the forecastle. Down that thing came.

"CRASH!

"Rolling upside down. Around and around. We rolled over twice. Around and around.

"Now I've lost all sense of direction. Pitch black. Blacker'n hell. You've ever got in a black closet with a wet cloth over your face and closed your eyes couldn't a been any blacker.

"Totally utter black. Totally utter lost all your directions. I didn't know if I was upside down, right side up. I didn't know where I was. I did know that I could hold my breath a long time. I did know I was running out of air. I'm thinkin', "Jesus! I've got a daughter at home. My wife's pregnant at home with the next one. I'll never get to see my next kid. I'll never know whether it's a boy or a girl.'

"Dammit! I just don't want to die like this. But, I just know this boat is sunk. I know it is sittin' upside down. I know I'm goin' ta stick my head right out of the sand. Boat's upside down on the bottom, so that when I stick my head up, my head will be right in the sand. That was my thought.

"But really the boat has almost a three ton keel and that would be the down part if we sunk and I would still be up. But at that moment I thought I was sunk upside down.

"But I said, 'I'M GOING FOR IT!'

"'Arraugh!" I stood up.

"God! Did that feel good! We were still floatin' right side up on the reef.

"Then, where's Nellie? I crawled across the forecastle and as I crawled I thought, 'What's all this line?' All wrapped in line. Then I remembered. 600 feet out in my stern, 350 feet from my anchor. Boat rolled completely around. Crawled across the forecastle. Black. Waitin' for the next breaker. We're goin' to go over again. We've got a whole reef to go over. We're goin' ta go over three or four more times. If it comes now, I'm gone. So, I get back to the coxswain area. The spray shield is all tore up, the radio is gone. Miller is gone. Six inches of wire is left from the searchlight – the searchlight is gone. I yelled out in the darkness, 'Oh, shit! What am I gonna do?'

"I'm by myself. Miller is gone. I can't help him. Save my ass, I guess. So, what do I do? Go out there and ride that hole again? Oh, God! I hate that. Should I go in the engine room? Should I duck under the catwalk? There's a place under the catwalk where you could duck and brace yourself against the walkway on top. I'm tryin' to think.

"I gotta go to one of those places. To survive this thing when it hits the beach.

"About that time I hear, 'MAC!' There's Miller.

Master Chief McAdams' cigars were almost as famous as he was. He only spat them out if the lifeboat he was driving was about to roll over. United States Coast Guard

"'MILLER!'

"'MAC!'

"Jesus! I reached over the side and there he is. Luckily I grabbed him. I grabbed him by the hair, the ears, the shoulders, and drug him over the side and dumped him on the well deck.

"He said, 'We rolled over!'

"'Yeah, I know.'

"I grabbed his ass. 'You're going underneath the catwalk by the towing bit. All you have to do is brace yourself. You brace yourself!'

"'Where you goin'?'

"'I'm goin' to the bow to see if the boat is comin'. I made a call. Maybe one of the other boats is comin'.' I looked up. 'Here come the runnin' lights. I'm going for it!'

"It was totally black. So, I crawled back up on the forecastle. Jumped in the hole again.

"And here comes the Depoe Bay boat.

"They got time enough to get us a line. And they have an extra man. THEY GOT THREE GUYS! The coxswain, the engineer, and do you know who the extra man was? A volunteer fireman! When you got a bad boat call at Depoe Bay – they only had a few people at the station – they'd blow the whistle and the volunteer fire department would send a man down. (The Coast Guard also helped the volunteer fire department.) The volunteer fireman, he was seasick. I don't know about the other guys.

"Well, we'd just put these nice stainless steel reels on the back of their boat. They would hold almost 900 feet of four-inch line. Big reel. You had a crank on one end and you had to crank it out or take it in. Well, I could still look out of the hole and see them. They yelled, 'We'll be back!'

"I don't believe it! I don't believe they're doin' their house keeping. I mean, there goes my ass!

"We take a breaker or two. We roll about 90 degrees. DOWN WE COME! Oh, God!

"Here they come! Here they come!

"It's the other lifeboat. He's outside of us, as we're being pushed inside. I watch him catch a breaker. He don't have a drogue or nothin'. He's coming' right for us. Like he's goin' ta cut us in two, 'cause he's skiin'. He's doin' fifteen or twenty knots on that breaker. He's got a searchlight. That's the only way I can see 'im. There's this light bouncing off of us and I can see his two runnin' lights.

"Oh, shit! He's goin' ta cut us right in two.

"About that time the drogue, the little drogue – BOOM – opens up and stops us. If I had been quicker, I could have jumped right from the bow hole right into his well deck. He was that close.

"Then he went over broadside. I seen him goin'. He almost went over. After we got back into the station, you could look into his engine room and see where the oil went up the bulkhead to just about the centerline and came back. He went. He had one man with him and he had the old battle lantern. He dropped it when he went over. I could see this battle lantern disappearing beneath the breakers. Curious thing. I could hear this engine choking off in the distance. I could see the light disappear. They're gone. Then I heard the engine catch and they've made it out of here.

"I went back and grabbed Miller and said, 'C'me, guy, we're all by ourselves. Let's go forward and lock ourselves in the forecastle. At least if we roll over we can breathe.'

"We went forward and opened the little hatch in the forecastle. Got in there. 'Grab some lifejackets!' There's a dim light in the overhead so you can see. 'Grab some lifejackets and start wrapping them around you!'

"I looked around and, Jesus! Some of the gear had come loose. God! Here's the axe! So I throw it out the hatch and grab two or three other things and threw them out the hatch.

"Two dogs (latches) on the hatch and I dogged the hatch back down. And you brace yourself in there.

"'Let's brace ourselves with all these life jackets!'

"Just about this time a breaker hit us. Oh, Jesus! Up and around we went. And over. Jesus! Lifejackets and shit is flying around. Something hit me on the top of my head. Oh, God! I reached up.

"Miller! DID YOU HIT ME ON THE HEAD?'

"NO, BUT YOU SURE ARE BLEEDIN'!'

"The old one-quart fire extinguisher got tore off the bulkhead. Hit me. With that aviation hat I had on, it skidded off. Took a hunk of hide the size of a quarter off my head. But you bleed like hell from a head wound. Of course, you're soaking wet. All this blood and all this water.

"'GOD! YOU SURE ARE BLEEDIN'!'

"So we rolled and then it got good for a while. We're inside the reef. All of a sudden we start takin' breaks.

"I said, 'You know, if we hit the beach, we'll let the surf push the boat. If we hit the jetty, the rocks are going to come right through this thing. I'm going to get rid of this fire extinguisher right now!'

"I went to open the hatch... moved the hatch two inches. It was jammed. Unbeknownst to the builders and unknown to anybody up to that time and the years of the 36-footer, if the ready box lid is partially opened the hatch ran into it. The hatch opened over the ready box. If the hatch was closed and the lid raised: 'Klunk!' So I reached over and grabbed the Very pistol.

"Miller yells, 'DON'T SHOOT IT! DON'T SHOOT IT!'

"I AIN'T GOING TA SHOOT IT! I'M GOING TO USE IT AS A PRY! YOU HIT THE HATCH!' He hit it with his shoulder and finally we got the right rhythm and the hatch flew open.

"I jumped up and grabbed the axe. I could see what happened. I started to cut the corner of the open ready box. Lookin' over my shoulder for the next break, because if it hits me now, I'm gone. It will also be flooded inside. I closed the hatch. I cut the end off the ready box lid. I almost cut through the watertight bulkhead. I dove back inside. Dogged down the hatch.

"We sat in there and told sea stories. It wasn't too long. We hit.

"'Let's get out of here!'

"'No, no,' I says. 'Its sand! It's sand! Are you a good swimmer?'

"'Oh, God! I can hardly swim at all.'

"'Okay, I'll take care of you. Here's what happens. We hit the beach. It won't be very deep. But there's potholes sometimes six-eight feet deep. When we get up on deck, I'll look it over and tell you when to jump. I'll jump right behind you. That way when you hit, I'll be there to grab you and we'll go.'

"'Okay.'

"'Okay, let's get out of here.'

"Well, you're about ten feet in the air. Even on the beach, when you're on those rolling chocks you're eight-ten feet in the air. I looked around and no potholes. Straight surf. Good sand.

"Okay hold it! Hold it! NOW!'

"Well, Jesus! Miller wasn't lookin'. He was sick and out of it. He took off like he was going to dive in the ocean. Took off in a half swan dive. Jesus! It was only three to five inches of water. He hit. BOOM! Big lifejacket on. Knocked the wind out of him.

"'I THOUGHT YOU SAID IT WAS GOING' TA BE DEEP!'

"'HELL, NO! LET'S GO!'

"I grabbed him by the ass and up the beach we went.

"I could see strange lights comin' down the beach. What it was, was Mr. Lawrence, our CO. He was comin' in the big Oshkosh. They crashed through the logs and got down on the beach. They're roaring up the beach and their headlights picked us up. He jumped down and came running to us.

"'How are you?'

"'We're fine.'

"'Fine. Fine. Let's get out of here.'

"Just as we hit the beach, sirens went off. New Year's, welcoming us back."

Master Chief Thomas D. McAdams and his engineer weren't the only survivors of that night's harrowing adventure. The 36-footer they rode on New Year's Eve 1953 now sits displayed on the lawn of the Yaquina Bay Station, Newport, Oregon.

1. I heard from another old salt that after the show aired sometimes when Tom received telephone calls and he identified himself, the caller would say "Woof! Woof!" and hang up.

2. The audio-taped interview was conducted at the Yaquina Bay Station in 1996 as research for the writing of *Lifeboats Sailors: The U.S. Coast Guard's Small Boat Stations*, Brassey's (Washington, D.C. 2000).

ABOUT THE AUTHORS

Paul Barnett is the author of the book *The Lifesaving Guns of David Lyle* and is the leading authority on Lyle guns in the United States. He is president and owner of South Bend Replicas of South Bend, Indiana, which manufactures rare antique cannons, including Lyle guns. Paul is well known for providing and firing the Lyle guns used during performances of Tchaikovsky's "1812 Overture" by many of the country's leading symphonies.

Frederick "Bud" Cooney enlisted in the U.S. Coast Guard immediately after graduation from La Salle Academy in Providence, Rhode Island in 1951. He served on active duty as a seaman and later as a radioman. He entered the Coast Guard Reserve program and retired a Lieutenant Commander with thirty-eight years of combined service and is now fully retired with his wife Ann in Charlestown, Rhode Island.

John J. Galluzzo is the editor of *Wreck & Rescue Journal*. Born in Hull, Massachusetts, the hometown of America's greatest lifesaver, Joshua James, he is a freelance writer contributing to newspapers and magazines throughout the South Shore of Boston area, with a focus on maritime history and modern day Coast Guard search and rescue stations. He has authored or coauthored twenty books on local history, and penned the first chapter of the Foundation for Coast Guard History's book, *Coast Guard*.

CDR Maurice E. Gibbs, USN (Ret.), is past president of the Nantucket Life-Saving Museum and past president of the U.S. Life-Saving Service Heritage Association. Commander Gibbs is named for his grandfather, who was a surfman in the USLSS and USCG.

Robert W. Haley M.D., was a retired anesthesiologist, with many years experience and interest in resuscitation, hypothermia and drowning. Dr. Haley completed research for the Hull Lifesaving Museum during his retirement, and lived, during part of the year, about a mile from the site of the *Ulrica* wreck. Dr. Haley passed away in June 2006.

Donna Hill is professor emeritus and former head of the education library, Hunter College, CUNY. She is the author and sometimes illustrator of books of fiction for adults as well as young people. Her most recent book is *Shipwreck Season*, a historical novel for early teens about the United States Life-Saving Service on Cape Cod in 1880.

Dewey Livingston is the park historian at Point Reyes National Seashore in California. He is the author of numerous books, including the historical narrative section of *The History and Architecture of the Point Reyes Lifeboat Station*, published in 1990 by the National Park Service.

Mary Miles is a freelance writer who lives on Nantucket. She writes often for local publications and is the author of six books about the island, including four children's books. She initially became interested in Keeper Chase when she discovered he had lived in the house where she now resides.

Dennis L. Noble is a retired Coast Guard senior chief with a doctorate in history from Purdue University. He is the author of several books on the history of the Coast Guard, including *That Others Might Live: The U.S. Life-Saving Service, 1878-1914*, *Lighthouses and Keepers: The U.S. Lighthouse Service and Its Legacy* and *Lifeboat Sailors: Disasters, Rescues and the Perilous Future of the Coast Guard's Small Boat Stations*.

William D. Peterson is the author of *Images of America: United States Life-Saving Service in Michigan* and a museum professional currently living and working in Montana. A native of northern Michigan, he has spent much of his life in proximity to the old life-saving and lifeboat stations of the Great Lakes.

William Quinn is the author of several books on Atlantic Coast shipwrecks, beginning in 1873 with his classic *Shipwrecks Around Cape Cod*. He spent more than thirty years as a professional television news photographer along the New England coast covering many disasters including the *Andrea Doria* sinking in 1956 and the grounding and the subsequent loss of the tanker *Argo* in 1976.

Ralph Shanks is the coauthor of *The United States Life-Saving Service: Heroes, Rescues and Architecture of the Early Coast Guard* (with Wick York); *Guardians of the Golden Gate: Lighthouses and Lifeboat Stations of San Francisco Bay* (with Lisa Shanks); and the author of *Lighthouses and Lifeboats of the Redwood Coast*. He served as editor of the first fifteen issues of *Wreck & Rescue Journal*, from which many of the articles in this book are drawn. Ralph and Lisa Woo Shanks reside in Novato, California.

Frederick Stonehouse is the third president of the United States Life-Saving Service Heritage Association and president of the Marquette Maritime Museum. He is the author of numerous books on the maritime history of the Great Lakes, including *Wreck Ashore: The United States Life-Saving Service on the Great Lakes*, *The Wreck of the Edmund Fitzgerald*, and *Great Lakes Crime*. He has appeared nationally on the *History Channel*, *Fox Family* and *National Geographic*.

ENDNOTES

One of Nature's Noblemen

1. Thomas Farel Heffernan, *Stove By a Whale* (Middletown, CT, Wesleyan Univ. Press: 1981). An account of the experiences of Walter Chase's grandfather, Owen Chase, survivor of the Nantucket whaleship *Essex* rammed and sunk by a bull sperm whale on Nov 20, 1820.

2. Edward A. Stackpole, *Life Saving Nantucket* (Nantucket, MA, Stern-Majestic: 1972), Chap. XVIII, p. 182.

3. Ibid.

4. Ibid, p. 186. As keeper of Coskata LSS, Chase had his surfboat painted red to be seen in the ice surrounding Nantucket in the winter. He was mindful of a *Muskeget LSS* crew that had nearly been lost in an earlier rescue. Their rescuers were unable to find them in the ice fields. Later (Feb. 1, 1918) *Cross Rip* Lightship was lost with its crew of six when ice ripped it from its moorings and swept it to sea.

5. Ibid., p. 187.

Brave Men of Hull

1. The strong ties of family and friendship in this small community continued as close cooperation between the Life-Saving Service and the Humane Society. After Joshua James transferred to the Life-Saving Service his son, Osceola, succeeded him as the Humane Society's Keeper in Hull, serving in this capacity until 1928.

2. "The Surfboat-Lifeboat *Nantasket*. Hull, Massachusetts. The boat that would not succeed." By Dennis R. Means. Reprinted from *The American Neptune*, Vol. XXXVII, No. 2, 1977. Copyright 1977 by the Peabody Museum, Salem, Massachusetts.

3. *The Boston Post*, December 17, 1896.

Association Information:
The United States Life-Saving Service Heritage Association
P.O. Box 213
Hull, Massachusetts 02045
www.us-lifesavingservice.org